BARR

NATHANIEL HAWTHORNE'S

The Scarlet Letter

BY

Sara Sheldon

SERIES EDITOR

Michael Spring
Editor, *Literary Cavalcade*
Scholastic Inc.

BARRON'S EDUCATIONAL SERIES, INC.

ACKNOWLEDGMENTS

We would like to acknowledge the many painstaking hours of work Holly Hughes and Thomas F. Hirsch have devoted to making the *Book Notes* series a success.

Copyright 1984 by Barron's Educational Series, Inc.

All inquiries should be addressed to:
Barron's Educational Series, Inc.
250 Wireless Boulevard
Hauppauge, New York 11788

Library of Congress Catalog Card No. 84-18422

International Standard Book No. 0-8120-3442-2

Library of Congress Cataloging in Publication Data
Sheldon, Sara.
  Nathaniel Hawthorne's The scarlet letter.

  (Barron's book notes)
  Bibliography: p. 113
  Summary: A guide to reading "The Scarlet Letter" with
a critical and appreciative mind encouraging analysis
of plot, style, form, and structure. Also includes
background on the author's life and times, sample tests,
term paper suggestions, and a reading list.
  1. Hawthorne, Nathaniel, 1804–1864. Scarlet letter.
[1. Hawthorne, Nathaniel, 1804–1864. Scarlet letter.
2. American literature—History and criticism] I. Title.
II. Series.
PS1868.S4   1984   813'.3   84-18422
ISBN 0-8120-3442-2 (pbk.)

PRINTED IN THE UNITED STATES OF AMERICA

23   550   98765

CONTENTS

ADVISORY BOARD

HOW TO USE THIS BOOK

You have to know how to approach literature in order to get the most out of it. This *Barron's Book Notes* volume follows a plan based on methods used by some of the best students to read a work of literature.

Begin with the guide's section on the author's life and times. As you read, try to form a clear picture of the author's personality, circumstances, and motives for writing the work. This background usually will make it easier for you to hear the author's tone of voice, and follow where the author is heading.

Then go over the rest of the introductory material—such sections as those on the plot, characters, setting, themes, and style of the work. Underline, or write down in your notebook, particular things to watch for, such as contrasts between characters and repeated literary devices. At this point, you may want to develop a system of symbols to use in marking your text as you read. (Of course, you should only mark up a book you own, not one that belongs to another person or a school.) Perhaps you will want to use a different letter for each character's name, a different number for each major theme of the book, a different color for each important symbol or literary device. Be prepared to mark up the pages of your book as you read. Put your marks in the margins so you can find them again easily.

Now comes the moment you've been waiting for—the time to start reading the work of literature. You may want to put aside your *Barron's Book Notes* volume until you've read the work all the way through. Or you may want to alternate, reading the *Book Notes* analysis of each section as soon as you have finished reading the corresponding part of the original. Before you move on, reread crucial passages you don't fully understand. (Don't take this guide's analysis for granted—make up your own mind as to what the work means.)

Once you've finished the whole work of literature, you may want to review it right away, so you can firm up your ideas about what it means. You may want to leaf through the book concentrating on passages you marked in reference to one character or one theme. This is also a good time to reread the *Book Notes* introductory material, which pulls together insights on specific topics.

When it comes time to prepare for a test or to write a paper, you'll already have formed ideas about the work. You'll be able to go back through it, refreshing your memory as to the author's exact words and perspective, so that you can support your opinions with evidence drawn straight from the work. Patterns will emerge, and ideas will fall into place; your essay question or term paper will almost write itself. Give yourself a dry run with one of the sample tests in the guide. These tests present both multiple-choice and essay questions. An accompanying section gives answers to the multiple-choice questions as well as suggestions for writing the essays. If you have to select a term paper topic, you may choose one from the list of suggestions in this book. This guide also provides you with a reading list, to help you when you start research for a term paper, and a selection of provocative comments by critics, to spark your thinking before you write.

THE AUTHOR AND HIS TIMES

It was a brash, bustling, energetic country in which Hawthorne grew up and carved out his writing career. The covered wagons were rolling West, with signs that bravely declared "California or bust!" The first passenger railroad opened, and the trains went huffing and puffing along at the (then) incredible speed of 20 miles an hour. Jackson was elected president, throwing the conservative statesmen out of office and ushering in the age of democracy and the common man.

It was an age between wars, when America, having beaten England for the second time—in the War of 1812—was flexing its adolescent muscles. Hope was in the air, and also a feeling of impatience with the imported, second-hand, European way of doing things. "Down with the past" might have been the slogan of the time. Americans sensed a fresh, creative task at hand in the building of a new country. It was a task that called for strong backs, clear eyes, and open minds.

There were experiments in living going on to match the experiments in politics and technology. Starry-eyed intellectuals gathered outside Boston to thrive on a vegetarian diet at Alcott's Fruitlands. Thoreau conducted his own private experiments in a life close to nature at Walden Pond. Horace Mann planned to change the world by changing education.

Where was Hawthorne while all this excitement was going on? In his bedroom in Salem, reading a book. You get the distinct feeling about this man that, so far as the great adventures of his time were concerned, he simply wasn't paying attention. Hawthorne was gazing intelligently off in another direction. Most of his generation looked expectantly toward the future. Hawthorne kept his eyes on the past.

He was an introvert, almost a recluse, this native son of Salem, Massachusetts. After graduating from Bowdoin College, he spent close to twelve years at home in his room, reading and learning his writer's craft. For subject matter, he turned not to life but to books and to his own family history. When he was a boy, his Puritan ancestors had haunted his imagination. And now, he read voraciously about early New England history, fleshing out his childhood dreams.

Perhaps Hawthorne read so much about the Puritans that their concerns became his. More likely, his reading struck a chord in him that was already familiar. Hawthorne thought about sin. He thought about guilt. He thought about the dark side of the soul. He pondered questions that few other men of his time thought or cared about—questions like: What happens to people who nurse a secret sin throughout their lives? Or, is it true that the evil taint of a crime lingers forever on the soul?

Hawthorne had a wide, unconventional streak in his soul, and he didn't like it. Some part of him was always at war with the recluse and pessimist in himself.

Hawthorne even briefly flirted with Utopianism. He joined Brook Farm, a community near Boston, in the hopes that a life in the open air, in communion with other writers, would be congenial to him. But milking cows and raking manure proved too much for Hawthorne. He left after a year to resume a private writing career.

Hawthorne made other attempts to put himself in touch with the currents of his time. At the age of 35, he sought—of all things—a political appointment. Hawthorne went to work in the Salem Custom House, where his nose was really rubbed in the grimy details of trade.

There was a good reason for that particular choice. Hawthorne had met his future wife, Sophia Peabody, and he needed money to marry on. He was never a best-selling author, and a lack of funds was a problem he would wrestle with all his life.

The question of money would rear its ugly head again in 1846 when Hawthorne, now a husband and a father, returned to the Salem Custom House as Surveyor. He spent three mildly discontented years there, to be thrown out in 1849 when a Whig victory ended the Democrats' reign. (Hawthorne was a member of the Democratic party.)

Hawthorne was bitter at such high-handed treatment. But his dismissal from the Custom House proved a blessing in disguise. He was free to write again. Indeed, he *had* to write in order to keep a roof over his head. He set immediately to work and produced *The Scarlet Letter*, published in 1850.

Perhaps the novel served as a kind of creative trigger, for the famous works now followed quickly, one on the heels of another: *The House of the Seven Gables* in 1851, and *The Blithedale Romance* in 1852.

We can talk about the later events of Hawthorne's life: the birth of more children, a consulship to England, the publication of *The Marble Faun* in 1860. And yet, if we do, we will get no closer to the man. Hawthorne lived a decent, middle-class, intellectual sort of life. He wrote, he served his country in minor capacities, he had children, he worked to support them. And yet, there was something he held back, a part of himself he showed only to the four walls of his room.

Nathaniel Hawthorne was a man, for instance, who married a genteel, delicate woman, a woman to whom love meant the sweet sound of violins. But the creator of Hester Prynne knew a different side of things; knew just as surely as he lived that there were dark, erotic temptresses out there with eyes a man could drown in.

THE NOVEL

The Plot

The year is 1642. The place is Boston, a small Puritan settlement. Before the town jail, a group of somber people wait with stern expressions on their faces. They are expecting Hester Prynne, a woman convicted of adultery and condemned to stand on the village scaffold for three hours of public shame.

Hester appears, carrying an infant in her arms, and wearing a scarlet letter *A* (for Adulteress) as a badge of her disgrace. A careful look at Hester's face, however, shows she is not contrite, as the crowd expects, but rather quietly defiant. Three hours on the scaffold do little to change her attitude. When pressed by the magistrates to repent of her crime and name her lover to the authorities, Hester answers with a silence that echoes through the market-place. She scorns her judges. To one man alone does she show any sign of fear.

That man is Hester's husband who has just arrived in town, having sent Hester ahead from Europe two years before. Taking quick stock of the situation, he disguises his identity and assumes a new one, that of Roger Chillingworth, physician. Before Hester's ordeal is over, Chillingworth has made his plans. He will stay in Boston and search out his unnamed rival.

That night, Chillingworth visits Hester in prison to secure her promise of secrecy. The world must not know him as her husband. Hester agrees to Chillingworth's demands, partly out of exhaustion, partly out of fear that her husband will indeed find and expose her lover. It is a promise she will live to regret.

The years go by. Hester, released from prison, moves with her daughter Pearl to a small cottage on the outskirts of town. There she earns a meager living as a seamstress. Though Hester's conduct is now quiet and modest, her life is made hell on earth by the unforgiving citizens of Boston who shun her, or insult her, as the woman of the scarlet letter.

There is even an attempt, led by the Governor himself, to take Hester's child from her. But the attempt fails when Hester goes to the Governor's mansion to fight in person for Pearl. There she enlists the aid of Arthur Dimmesdale, the colony's revered young minister, who argues convincingly on Hester's behalf.

In the meantime, Chillingworth has made quite a name for himself as a doctor. He has approached Dimmesdale, who is not well, with an offer of his services. Dimmesdale is gently pressured into accepting medical treatment. And Chillingworth takes the opportunity to cement first a professional relationship and then an intimate friendship with the minister.

What is Chillingworth up to? He has his suspicions that Dimmesdale is the man he is looking for, the man who should have stood by Hester's side on the scaffold. Chillingworth now watches, listens, tests, and probes, until he finds what he is looking for: an *A* on Dimmesdale's chest (we might call it a psychosomatic sign) just like the letter worn by Hester Prynne.

Dimmesdale is the guilty man; he is also a guilt-ridden one. The secret the minister carries within him is burning to get out. He starts to confess in his sermons, but cowardice holds him back. He reels to the scaffold to stand vigil where Hester has stood and goes to the telltale spot, unseen, in the dead of night.

Dimmesdale's torment is increased by Chillingworth, who takes his revenge by playing on the minister's guilt. It is Hester who calls a halt to the physician's ugly game. She has seen how suffering has wasted Dimmesdale away. She accuses herself of leaving him—unknowing and unaware—a victim in her estranged husband's hands.

Hester meets Dimmesdale in the forest to tell him the truth about Chillingworth. The meeting reawakens passionate feelings in them both. Hester and Dimmesdale plan to escape. They will go to England, where Chillingworth cannot follow, and there they will build a new and better life.

Between the meeting in the forest and the day planned for escape, however, something snaps in Dimmesdale. The minister has a change of heart. He is a dying man, and he knows it. He holds himself together long enough to give the most triumphant sermon of his life. Then he mounts the scaffold (this time in daylight) to confess his sin and to die in Hester's arms.

The story has a postscript. Chillingworth dies with his victim and leaves his money to—of all people— Pearl. Hester and her daughter leave New England for Europe, where Pearl marries an aristocrat. Hester, now alone, returns to Boston where she resumes, of her own accord, the scarlet letter. Years later, when she dies, she is buried in a grave next to the minister's, where one tombstone, with an engraved letter *A*, serves for them both.

The Characters

Hester Prynne

Hester Prynne is one of the most enigmatic characters in all literature. As the wearer of the scarlet letter, she may be expected to possess some definitive insight available to no one else. Yet her final word on the subject is "I know not. I know not."

Is Hester a glorious heroine, standing up to an unduly repressive society in the name of love and freedom? Or is she a sinner who has broken a basic and sacred law? And if she is a sinner, does sin lead her in the direction of evil or of good?

Let's look at Hester from a number of different viewpoints:

1. Hester is a magnificent woman fighting for her natural rights to love and freedom. To know what Hawthorne means by his heroine, you have only to look at her. With her flashing eyes, her rich complexion, and her abundant hair, she stands for what a real woman should be beside a crowd of tight-mouthed Puritans.

It is true that during the years of her punishment, Hester tries to subdue her spirit and sensuality, hiding it all (with that wonderful hair of hers) beneath a sad cap. But she can't do it. One breath of fresh air, one ray of sunlight, one moment alone with her lover in the forest, and she is herself again, reaching passionately for a life of freedom and fulfillment.

2. Hester Prynne, if not the out-and-out criminal the Puritans believe her to be, is still a woman who has deeply sinned. She is, after all, guilty of adultery—no small matter, even today.

As Hester herself admits, she has irreparably wronged her husband. And so she bears some responsibility for the corruption of Chillingworth's soul.

She has also shattered Dimmesdale's peace. She has lured the minister—admittedly, with his full cooperation—from the straight and narrow path of orthodoxy, where it was surely in his interest to stay.

3. Hester is, indeed, a sinner. But her sin is a cause not of evil but of good. Suffering disciplines Hester, so that she grows strong. Sorrow awakens her sympathies, so that she becomes a nurse.

In fact, the best deeds of Hester's life come about through her fall from grace. Her charity to the poor, her comfort to the broken-hearted, her unquestioned presence in times of trouble are the direct result of her search for repentance. If Hester had not sinned, she would never have discovered the true depths of tenderness within herself.

4. Hester is neither a heroine nor a sinner, but something in between. She is a flesh-and-blood woman in tragic circumstances, trapped in a loveless marriage and in love with another man. Whichever way she moves, there is bound to be a sacrifice of some vital part of herself, either her honor or her deepest need.

Arthur Dimmesdale

Dimmesdale is a coward and a hypocrite. Worse, he is a self-confessed coward and hypocrite. He knows what he has to do to still the voice of his conscience and make his peace with God. He simply cannot bring himself to do it.

Dimmesdale is somewhat pale and weak from the first moment we see him. And he grows paler and weaker by the minute, as he lives ridden with guilt, a guiltmonger by his side. By the time the minister comes to the forest, he barely has the strength to throw himself down on the leaves in the hope that he can lie there forever. He lacks the will even to wish to live or die.

When we read such a description, we cannot help wondering what Hester ever saw in the man.

Yet there is a presence in the minister that demands a live audience and knows how to sway one. We see it in his eyes—large, brown, and melancholy—which seem to search out men's souls. We hear it in his voice—sweet, deep, broken—a finely tuned instrument for touching women's hearts.

Were Dimmesdale just a little stronger, a little more energetic, we would say he has charisma. And probably, in his own time and place, he did. Ministers were the Puritan culture's heroes. Hester would have met Dimmesdale first as the revered idol of the community, the object of worshipping glances from every girl in sight.

We sense in Dimmesdale this split between his private and his public self, his purity and his passion. We wonder, was the split always there?

To some extent, Dimmesdale's story is the story of any sensitive young man's initiation into sexuality, especially in a society that treats sexuality with ill grace. But his problem is enormously complicated by the fact of Hester's marriage (for him no technicality), and by his own image of himself as a cleric devoted to higher things. Unlike other young men, Dimmesdale cannot accept his loss of innocence and go on from there. He must struggle futilely to get back to where he was.

By the time we meet Dimmesdale, he has lost (if he ever had it) the simplicity of an earlier time. He has bitten into the apple and destroyed his old sense of oneness with God. The split in the man's nature is deepened by his situation. If he wishes to continue in his ministerial role, he must bury his sensuality and wrap himself up in a cloak of sanctity. He must wear one face for the world, another for himself.

What happens to a man who struggles to hide a terrible sin in the depths of his heart, but who believes profoundly in a God that sees and loves the truth? That is a question Hawthorne surely asked himself in creating the character of Arthur Dimmesdale.

If the minister is a brilliant study in guilt, it is because he believes with all his soul that his sin *is* terrible, and that a concerned, personal God is watching every move he makes.

Torn between the desire to confess and atone and the cowardice which holds him back, Dimmesdale goes a little mad. He takes up some morbid forms of penance—fasts and scourgings—but he can neither whip nor starve the sin from his soul. In his agony, he staggers to the pulpit to confess, but his words come out as generalized, meaningless avowals of guilt.

Dimmesdale knows what he is doing, of course. "Subtle, but remorseful, hypocrite," he is nothing if not self-aware. But the dark stain he perceives on his soul is spreading now, sapping the meaning from life, the strength from his will.

By the time the minister meets Hester in the forest, he is ripe for an invitation to flight. Perhaps flight is the only way out. And anyway, he wonders, for a moral wreck like himself, what does it really matter whether he goes or stays?

If he stays, there is Chillingworth, whose gloating eye he does not know how to escape. There is duty, too, that endless round of tasks he has always gone about without complaint. But the tasks seem hollow now, since (as he believes) he is unfit for his office, since his actions are no longer informed by any sustaining faith.

If he goes, there is Hester and the dream of love he has not permitted himself for so long. A glowing face in the firelight and an embrace (has he not just felt it?) that is like an infusion of strength. There is England, too, with the sweet, deep-sounding bells of Cambridge, and the winters soft after New England's penetrating cold. And minds of his own calibre! The chance, after nine or ten years, to really talk!

Dimmesdale nearly buys the shining vision of a new life that Hester holds out to him in the woods. And yet, with his last ounce of strength, he rejects it. He crawls to the scaffold—and confession—instead.

Is Dimmesdale right to choose confession over escape; the shreds of his religious belief over Hester and love? Your answer will depend on your own definition of the good life, and on where you think Dimmesdale has been headed all along.

Some readers believe that Dimmesdale's decision is the only possible ending to his long and tortuous struggle to return to God. Others see it as a desperate flight from his true, but never acknowledged, self.

Let's look at the second argument first. According to this view, Dimmesdale found out something essential about himself when he fell in love with, and made love to, Hester Prynne. He found out he was not a pure, ethereal scholar-priest, but a man with a man's heart and a man's desires. What should he have done about it? What all men do, when they are ready to grow up. Accept responsibility for a wife and child. Marry the woman (or live with her, in this case) and keep a roof over her head.

The first argument runs somewhat differently. The real Dimmesdale (it goes) is no lover at all, but a Puritan minister from the top of his head to the tips of his toes. In Hester's arms, he may have yielded temporarily to the claims of the flesh. But he never altered his basic commitment to the spirit, and to God. The point is not whether *we* belive that Dimmesdale's love for Hester is sin. The point is that *he* believes it, with all his heart. There is only one way he can expiate that sin. And that is to stand on the scaffold and confess.

The chilling fact about either argument is that it leaves half of Dimmesdale out. The flesh has to go or the spirit. There is no way of integrating both. Dimmesdale is given a stark choice, and he is given it by Hawthorne: To deny love and desire (and their consequent human commitments) in the only final way possible, in death; or to live, and submerge his finer qualities in a life too closely tied to earth.

Roger Chillingworth

Sometime in your study of literature, you've probably heard the distinction between flat characters and characters in the round. Round characters, or three-dimensional ones, leap out from the page with all the vigor and complexity of life. Flat characters, or two-dimensional ones, stay firmly imbedded in the work of which they are a part. Flat characters have a specific literary task to perform. They never get away from their function long enough to assume a life and a will of their own.

The distinction between flat and round characters is important with regard to Roger Chillingworth because most critical discussions address the question of just how convincing a character he is. He is, in part, an evil type that Hawthorne has used in his fiction before: the cold heart that observes and does not feel. (As the character's name implies, Chillingworth is worth a chill.) But does he ever become anything more than a type? Does he, like Hester and Dimmesdale, take on human dimensions?

There are two radically different answers to that question. You will have to decide between them.

1.   To some readers, Chillingworth is a creature right out of melodrama. Hawthorne might have borrowed him from a grade-B horror film. Chillingworth's very appearance is a hackneyed convention for villainy. A misshapen shoulder—shades of Richard III! As if that weren't enough, there are Chillingworth's smoldering eyes and his dark, sooty face. Why, the man is even less than a real villain. He is an imaginary fiend.

Chillingworth's appearance aside, his very singleness of purpose is inhuman. For seven years, he has only one thought: to find and torment the man who has betrayed him. Now who is there among us who eats, sleeps, dreams, and breathes revenge?

2.   Other readers say that, despite the demonic imagery surrounding him, Chillingworth remains very much a man. He is, after all, a wronged husband, a figure the 17th century held up to ridicule and abuse. His lust for revenge is therefore not unnatural, and his method of revenge not hackneyed at all. No sword or poison for Chillingworth. He takes the psychological approach.

There are also hints in Chillingworth of a character more complex than any simple, straightforward villain would be. He has the gift of irony, for instance. And by turning the cool light of irony on himself, he is able to share the blame for Hester's infidelity. The learned scholar, as he says to himself, should have seen it coming, should have read about it in his books.

The really interesting question about Chillingworth is why Hawthorne felt he had to clamp down on this character, hammer him into place with nails, and slap a label of "fiend" upon him. Why didn't he just leave Chillingworth free to grow in life and reality, the way he left Hester Prynne? The answer seems to lie in Hawthorne's terror of Chillingworth's hungry and far-reaching mind.

Chillingworth, we must recognize, is a brilliant scientist. It is no accident that the doctor takes Boston by storm. He has the capacity—rare in any age, unheard of in Puritan New England—to observe the world without preconceptions, and then to put his observations to work.

Consider. Chillingworth finds himself beached after a shipwreck, a prisoner among the Indians. What does he do? Does he turn up his nose at a pack of half-naked savages? Does he mutter incantations against demons and black magic? Does he even quote to the uncomprehending red man passages from the Bible or from European medical texts? Not at all. Chillingworth considers the possibility that the Indians may have something to teach him. And he sets himself to learn New World medicine from the Medicine Man.

It is amazing, really. Just how amazing, we can see by comparing Dimmesdale and Chillingworth. How alike the two men are, and yet how different!. Both are scholars, somewhat too committed to midnight oil and dusty books. But Dimmesdale is orthodox. Eventually, he shies away from new and upsetting ideas to seek refuge in his faith.

Chillingworth, on the contrary, has a brave and adventurous mind. He has profited from life in post-Renaissance Europe. He has seen nature yielding its secrets to the scientific method. He knows that the future belongs to him and to men of his kind.

And yet, Chillingworth's is a mind untempered by mercy, humanity, or compassion. He is all head and no heart. His probing intellect, as we know from his dealings with Dimmesdale, recognizes no "Stop" or "Caution" sign.

Pearl

Pearl. She is Hester's treasure, the pearl of great price, purchased with her mother's peace of mind and position in society.

Pearl. She is no treasure to the critics. She has caused many a reader to recommend murder as the only way to deal with such a maddening character.

What is it about Pearl that gets normally sober men and women so riled up? The character presents problems because we can never relax and enjoy her as a normal child. We must always be on the alert for what she *means*.

Pearl is a fascinating experiment, an attempt by Hawthorne to yolk a symbol to a human being and make them live comfortably together in one body. Sometimes the experiment is successful. Sometimes it's a flop. Let's look at two scenes in *The Scarlet Letter* that represent the two ends of the spectrum. Where does Pearl "work"?

She works particularly well in the forest scene in the chapter called "The Child at the Brook-Side." If you look at Pearl's actions here, they are perfectly understandable without any symbolic interpretation.

She cries, she stamps her feet in the resentment any child would feel at seeing a proper and decorous mother suddenly blossom into sexuality. Little girls don't like sexy mothers suddenly thrust upon them. Nor do they welcome brand-new and unexpected fathers. Pearl is saying what any petted, spoiled child would say under the circumstances: either you love him (that strange, sad man over there), or you love me.

In the forest scene, the real child can carry the symbol, because Pearl's narrative meaning and her symbolic meaning so neatly coincide. The child points an accusing finger at Hester, and so does fate. The child says, go and pick your own letter up. And fate echoes, the scarlet letter is your burden to carry and yours alone. We feel the magic of the double role, but not the strain.

Now let's look at a more gruesome incident, Pearl's first appearance in her tunic of crimson and gold. We know, because Hawthorne has told us, that Puritan children just don't run around dressed that way.

Admittedly, Pearl is no run-of-the-mill Puritan child. She is the daughter of an outcast, a renegade. But whatever Hester is, she loves her daughter and wants to keep her. And in order to keep Pearl, Hester has to prove her conformity to the grimmest and sternest of Puritan magistrates. It is hardly proof of conformity to arrive at the Governor's mansion, where everyone will be dressed in black, with a little girl outrageously decked out in scarlet. (Suppose Dimmesdale hadn't been around to explain?)

There is a tug-of-war going on here between Pearl's symbolic function and the psychological demands of the story. Unless we make a great imaginative effort, we simply don't believe what is going on. We are distracted, so to speak, by the creaking of the symbolic machinery.

Mistress Hibbins

Mistress Hibbins is a witch. Come on, you'll say, there is no such thing as a witch. Not around the corner from your house, perhaps. But there were witches in 17th-century Boston. Or, at least, there were women who thought they were witches and who conversed regularly with the devil.

Mistress Hibbins, as the Governor's sister and a woman of birth and breeding, raises an interesting question. Why would a lady of means and education choose to be known as a witch, when she was likely to end up at the stake?

Probably the principal appeal of witchcraft lay in its freedom. Alone among the women of this rigid, strait-laced society, witches could say and do as they liked.

They could express violent hatred, blatant sexual desire, and a slew of other emotions virtuous women had to suppress. Above all, witches enjoyed a rare privilege in a society that buried so many things—the privilege of telling the truth.

As you will see, Mistress Hibbins not only says what she likes. What she has to say is right. She has a sharp nose for secrets, this elegant old hag. She knows just which shy virgins or modest young deacons have been dancing in the forest, when Somebody was the fiddler.

Now, truth can be a nuisance. Who wants to be reminded all the time of midnight deeds and secret thoughts? The historical Mistress Hibbins, on whom the fictional character is based, was, in fact executed for witchcraft in 1656.

Other Elements

SETTING

There are two ways to talk about setting in *The Scarlet Letter*. One way is to look at the meaning or emotional overtones of specific places. A second and broader way is to examine the whole Puritan world in which Hawthorne has set his novel. Not just the time and place, Boston in the 1640s, but the values and beliefs that define Puritan society.

The Market-Place and the Forest
Far and away the most important scenes in *The Scarlet Letter* take place in two locations, the market-place and the forest. These are presented to us as very different places, reflecting very different human aspirations.

The market-place is public. It lies at the very heart of the tiny enclave of civilization the Puritans have managed to carve out of the vast, untouched continent. The market-place contains both the church and the scaffold—institutions of law and religion. It is where criminals like Hester are punished, where penitents like Dimmesdale confess, and where men put on the faces they wear for the world.

The forest, on the other hand, is dark and secret. It is where people come to let loose and be themselves. The forest track leads away from the settlement out into the wilderness where all signs of civilization vanish. The forest track is precisely the escape route from the dictates of law and religion to the promised land to the west where men can breathe free.

The market-place and the forest are symbols of the choice that confronts the major characters in the novel. The choice is not as simple as it seems.

For all its restraints, the market-place is safer and warmer than the forest. And you can't get into so much trouble there. In the heart of the settlement, there is the comfort of values that are shared, of laws that are laid down and respected. Above all, there is the comfort of people who care.

The open air of the forest is exhilarating, but cold. Nothing is known in the wilderness, everything is up for grabs. There is no one around to stop you from going to the devil. And when you do, he is right there waiting for you.

The Puritan World

Surely the setting of *The Scarlet Letter*—the stern, joyless world of Puritan New England—is one of the grimmest on record. It is all gloom and doom. If the sun ever shines, we hardly notice. The whole place seems shrouded in black. A question comes to mind as we read the novel. Why did Hawthorne choose this dark world for his masterpiece?

Perhaps we can tackle that question by asking another one. Why did Hawthorne reject the contemporary scene? Even if he chose to ignore the richly suggestive American settings of the 1820s and '30s, (the Erie Canal, for instance, or the Alamo), he had first-hand material to draw on in his own life and career.

Part of the answer, of course, is that Hawthorne *could* write about the contemporary scene. He *did* write about it in "The Custom House." But what he could write was comedy. The pathetic old Salemites who worked for Uncle Sam lent themselves not at all to the tragic work he had in mind.

Perhaps if Hawthorne reached back to Salem in the 1600s, he would find more figures invested with the same dark and dusky grandeur, more men and women who would speak as directly to his creative imagination.

The Puritan world of the mid-17th century apparently gave Hawthorne something he badly needed— people who lived their lives to the full instead of snoring them away. In the pages of *The Scarlet Letter*, the Puritans emerge from the shadows of an earlier time, broad shouldered, ruddy cheeked, firm of step, and direct of speech.

They were a stern people, of course, and repressive. They probably put the lid on more natural human impulses and emotions than any society before or since. But just for that reason, emotions boiled over, passions a novelist could seize at red heat.

More important, the Puritans had a moral vitality never again found on the American scene. For a writer like Hawthorne, intrigued with the subject of conscience, here were people with conscience to spare.

Whatever their faults, the Puritans at least knew the difference between right and wrong. And that was the sensibility Hawthorne was after.

THEMES

Law vs. Nature

We live in a permissive society. By and large, the law only bothers us when we bother the other guy. There is no law to tell us what to wear, how to think, or whom to love. In Puritan New England, life was vastly different. There, laws covered just about every aspect of life. Not surprisingly, human nature rebelled against such strict supervision. Certain impulses and emotions, passion foremost among them, would not be denied.

In the love of Hester and Dimmesdale, Hawthorne tells the story of one such rebellion. In a very real sense, the lovers are criminals. Their passion is a violation of the rigid Puritan civil and religious code. As wild as the forest which shelters it, the love of Hester and Dimmesdale asks us to weigh the justice of society's laws against the claims of human nature; that is, against men and women's most deeply felt desires and needs.

The Individual vs. Society

The individual *vs.* society. Law *vs.* nature. These are really just different terms for the same basic conflict. Hawthorne is a Romantic writer with a Romantic subject: a rebel who refuses to conform to society's code. Most of us instinctively side with the rebel, the nonconformist. But society in this novel has a good deal to be said for it. It has assurance, dignity, strength. We can argue that Hester is right in her assertion that fulfillment and love are worth fighting for. And we can argue, with just as much validity, that society is right in its joyless insistence that adultery is a crime deserving of punishment.

Sin and Redemption

Hawthorne, as a descendant of Puritans of the deepest dye, is the heir to a strong tradition of sin. Puritan theology began with the thoroughgoing conviction of sin. After Adam's fall, every man and woman was thought to be born an awful and vile sinner, who could be redeemed only by God's grace (not by good deeds or by any actions which lay within human control).

Now, Hawthorne is a 19th-century man of enlightenment. He is not a Puritan. Nevertheless, he is, morally speaking, something of a chip off the old block. As a writer, he is utterly immersed in sin, in the wages of sin, in the long odds on redeeming sin.

The Scarlet Letter is a study of the effects of sin on the hearts and minds of Hester, Dimmesdale, and Chillingworth. In every case, the effect is devastating. Once these characters stumble into evil, they flounder about as if in a morass. Sin changes the sinners. It darkens their vision and weakens the spirit's defenses against further temptation.

And yet, sin also pays some unexpected dividends. Sin strengthens Hester. It humanizes Dimmesdale. Hawthorne, departing from his Puritan ancestors, considers the possibility that sin may be a maturing force.

If sin is an encompassing shadow in the *The Scarlet Letter*, redemption is, at best, a fitfully shimmering light. Chillingworth never seeks redemption at all. Hester looks for it in good works, and fails to find it.

Dimmesdale alone undergoes the necessary change of heart to find a doubtful peace.

The Heart vs. the Head

Is there really a war waging inside us between our emotions and our reason? Hawthorne thinks so, and he's pretty sure which side he wants to win. The heart leads Hester and Dimmesdale astray, but the intellect—untempered by feeling, mercy, humanity—thoroughly damns Chillingworth. Hawthorne comes down on the side of the heart.

The Public and the Private Self

Hawthorne's Puritan New England is a world which encourages duplicity. So much is forbidden that almost everyone has something to hide. Hawthorne's characters walk around in daylight with pious and sober expressions on their faces. But once they get home at night and lock the door, they pull out their secret thoughts and gloat over them like misers delighting in a hidden stash of gold.

SYMBOLISM

Let's talk a little bit about what a symbol is. The common definition says that a symbol is a sign or token of something. A lion, for instance, is a symbol of courage. The bald eagle is a symbol of America. A white bridal gown is (or used to be) a symbol of purity. We take symbols like these pretty much for granted. They are a part of our everyday experience.

In literature, matters are a little more complicated. Literary symbols usually don't have instantly recognizable meanings. Rather they take their meanings from the works of which they are a part.

In *The Scarlet Letter*, Hawthorne gives us a symbol, a red letter A whose meaning has to be deciphered. What does the scarlet letter mean? It is a question repeated by almost every character in the novel who is confronted with the blatant red token and who has to deal with it: by Hester herself, as she sits in prison, decorating the emblem with golden thread; by Reverend Wilson, who addresses the crowd at the scaffold with such terrifying references to the scarlet A that it seems to glow red with hellfire; by Pearl, who asks about the letter so often that she threatens to drive her mother (and all of us) mad.

The symbol's meaning is hard to pin down because it is no passive piece of cloth, but a highly active agent. The scarlet letter provokes hostile feelings in the citizens of Boston, who shun Hester and insult her as something tainted and vile.

Society's response to the letter, in turn, affects Hester. On the surface, she becomes a patient and penitential figure. She *looks like* someone seeking to live down the sin that the scarlet letter represents. But beneath the surface, rebellion is brewing. Society's insults make Hester angry and bitter. She becomes a scornful critic of her world. Hester takes the letter to herself. She becomes in fact the renegade she is labeled. Hester breaks free of conventional ideas and, as we see in the forest scene, she opposes Puritan truths with some devastating truths of her own.

The point Hawthorne is making is that our lives are inevitably shaped by our past actions and by the signs of those actions—be they medals or badges of infamy—which we wear. Symbols like the scarlet letter shape our perceptions and our temperaments. They determine the kind of people we become.

Over the years, the scarlet letter and its wearer blend into one. The letter, whatever it means, is the summation of Hester's life. But a letter is a remarkably ambiguous symbol. It can stand for any word beginning with *A*.

Does the *A* stand for Adulteress, surely the intention of the magistrates who imposed it in the first place? Does it stand for Able in recognition of Hester's devotion as a nurse? Does it even mean Angel, with the consequent suggestion that Hester has risen above the society which condemned her?

There is danger and excitement in the uncertainty. If we knew for sure that the *A* stood for Adulteress, we would have Hester neatly pegged. We would know we were supposed to condemn her. But Hawthorne is not content to let the matter rest at that. He asks us to look at Hester from other, very different, viewpoints. We are never altogether sure whether we should condemn Hester or admire her.

STRUCTURE

The Scarlet Letter began life as a short story. (Hawthorne was advised to expand it into a novel, which he did.) In many respects, it retains the characteristics of a short story. *The Scarlet Letter* has the tightness and the economy we generally associate with the shorter fictional form.

Hawthorne's novel has only one plot. There are no subplots—no secondary love stories, for instance, such as you find in the novels of Jane Austen. It also has only one setting: Boston in the 1640s. Although Pearl and Hester eventually sail off to Europe, the reader is not invited to follow them there.

The Scarlet Letter has only four main characters: Hester, Dimmesdale, Chillingworth, and Pearl. All the other characters are really part of the historical tapestry against which the action takes place.

Perhaps most important of all, *The Scarlet Letter* has one predominating mood. For this, the lighting is largely responsible. We move in a world of darkness which is relieved only occasionally by a ray of light. (The darkness sets in early, with the beadle's presence obscuring the sunshine in Chapter 2. It continues to the end of the novel, with the legend on Hester's tombstone: "so somber . . . and relieved only by one ever-glowing point of light, gloomier than the shadow.")

Since Hawthorne's novel is such a spare and unified work, it is curious that readers disagree about its heart or structural center. Some critics believe that the heart of the book's structure is the scaffold, or penitential platform, to which Dimmesdale finally brings himself to stand by Hester's side. According to this view, the scaffold scenes alternate with the pivotal forest scenes, where the lovers confront the critical choice of escape from society or return to it.

But no less an authority than Henry James (the novelist's novelist and the acknowledged master of form in American fiction) disagrees. James dismisses the forest scenes—and indeed, any of the scenes where Hester plays a major part—as secondary. *The Scarlet Letter*, James says, is no love story. It is the story of retribution. And its center is the relationship between Dimmesdale and Chillingworth, the guilty lover and the sinister husband whose sole purpose is to keep that guilt alive.

The Story

THE CUSTOM HOUSE:
INTRODUCTORY

Unless you are specifically assigned otherwise, you should save "The Custom House" until after you have finished reading *The Scarlet Letter*.

Frankly, you will find the introduction rough going. It is long. It is plotless. It depends for its effect on a sense of humor that is far removed from modern comedy shows like *Saturday Night Live*. In addition, "The Custom House" is not really an integral part of the novel proper. It was added by Hawthorne as an afterthought on the advice of his publisher. The piece was supposed to add a light touch to an otherwise heavy work, and thereby increase sales.

"The Custom House" purports to be an explanation of how Hawthorne came to write *The Scarlet Letter*. In fact, you can read the piece twice over without discerning the truth. Hawthorne was fired from his job as Custom House Surveyor when the election of 1849 ousted his party from office. As the Custom House was a political appointment which depended on the good graces of the administration, Hawthorne was out of work.

In a way, the Custom House job did lead Hawthorne to *The Scarlet Letter*. The losing of it drove the novelist back to his original trade. What's more, Hawthorne's appointment as Surveyor brought him back to Salem. It put him, once again, in touch with his roots.

Salem had a firm hold on Hawthorne, even if it was a hold he sometimes struggled to break. The place had been native soil to his family for generations.

Hawthorne's father had been born there, and his father before him—sailors all, who helped to build the great New England shipping trade. And there were earlier and grander Hawthornes than that: John Hathorne (the *w* came later), the notorious hanging judge of the Salem Witch Trials; and John's father, William, one of the original founders of the colony, who had come over from England with Governor Winthrop in 1630.

In short, Hawthorne's roots in Salem went back just about as far as American history. On the western side of the Atlantic, that ranks as quite a family tree.

It was not the present Salem, however, with its decayed wharf and its equally decrepit inhabitants, that gripped Hawthorne's imagination. It was the town as it used to be: the bustling 18th-century port where the white-sailed clippers came to rest after their long voyages to the Indies, and the 17th-century village where grim-faced Puritans, swathed in black, trod the narrow streets with Bible in hand.

How could Hawthorne reach back into Salem's past and mine this rich vein for the characters and stories he wanted to write about? The Custom House pointed the way. The place, with its ancient officials, turned out to be a sort of local archives.

Hawthorne found that his co-workers, if they chose, had some fascinating stories to tell. The General, for instance, had fought in his youth in the War of 1812. He had even become a legend in his own time by uttering, when ordered to charge a British battery, a simple but courageous phrase. "I'll try, sir," the young officer had replied.

On a more mundane level, the Inspector also had a positive genius for summoning up the past. Why, the man could recall gourmet dinners he had eaten sixty or seventy years ago! As an appetizer, the Inspector was better than an oyster. He could make your mouth water with descriptions of long-since-devoured turkeys and roasts.

The officials aside, the Custom House itself was a repository of the past. On the second floor, a little-used cobweb-covered room housed a collection of ancient records. One day, while rummaging through the rubbish heaps, Hawthorne found a small package, neatly wrapped in yellowing parchment. It had apparently been overlooked by generations of previous Custom House employees.

Unwrapping the package, Hawthorne found "a certain affair of fine red cloth," shaped like the letter *A*. And along with that curious piece of cloth, he discovered a manuscript, which upon examination proved to date from Colonial times, recording the story of Hester Prynne.

Such, at any rate, is the story Hawthorne tells, for the discovery of the letter and the manuscript is a fabrication. Or perhaps, it is a metaphor for a far less poetic truth. The Custom House job was a relatively undemanding one that left Hawthorne with a lot of time on his hands. He used that time to continue his exhaustive research into the history of early New England. And in that research, or rather in the blend of historical fact with his creative imagination, Hawthorne found the story of *The Scarlet Letter*.

If the Custom House gave Hawthorne the chance to find his subject matter, it also gave him a stiff case of writer's block. Hawthorne couldn't write while he was still employed as Surveyor. There were too many distractions, too many petty details to attend to, too much jobbing and inefficiency about the place. The

Custom House was no atmosphere for a Romantic writer. Hawthorne needed, as he recognized, a more ethereal ambiance of moonbeams and firelight.

Perhaps we may see "The Custom House" as a sign of departure in American literature. Hawthorne was working his way out of a realistic tradition. He was reaching—it was the subject of every one of his prefaces—for a special blend of the actual and the imaginary. The imaginary is what pulled Hawthorne away from sunlit contemporary scenes, where the details were too sharp and clear, toward ancient shadowy places: prisons, castles, primeval forests. (Poe had arrived there shortly before him.)

Hawthorne would later distinguish between the novel, a type of work closely tied to historical fact, and the romance, a slightly different genre that gave the creative writer more elbow room. He would position himself as a writer of romances and demand all the license that the term bestowed.

There is another sense in which we can see "The Custom House" as a break with tradition. When he wrote the essay, Hawthorne was being anti-Progressive, critical of commerce, skeptical about the American dream. His was not the usual optimistic note of American writers. Only fifty years before, for example, Benjamin Franklin had gloried in the financial opportunities offered by the New World. He had chosen for his subject what we now call upward mobility. Here in America—unheard of in Europe—was the chance for a son to rise above his father's station in life.

Franklin fairly oozed with confident assurance that people could better themselves through hard work and perseverance. "The early bird catches the worm."

"A penny saved is a penny earned." Listen to Poor Richard, and you were practically guaranteed success in life.

Hawthorne was not of Franklin's mind. He was not an optimist. He distrusted easy guarantees. And he questioned the whole definition of success when it was presented to him in economic terms. For Hawthorne, commerce was not the upward climb to affluence. It was the path of descent from higher concerns.

We can see Hawthorne's slant in "The Custom House." His contemporary Salem fostered, not financial growth, but spiritual decay. Once New England's trade had smacked of adventure. But now the old sailors sat on the Custom House porch, warming their hides in the spring sun. Wards of the government, they had lost the vitality which characterizes men who live by their own efforts. They had sunk, in their dotage, into corruption and laziness.

Even the one efficient man in the outfit—shall we call him the Clerk or the Accountant? Hawthorne gives him no title—tended to confuse good bookkeeping with good morals. His integrity was really a matter of fastidiousness. A stain on his conscience would bother him in much the same way as an ink blot in his accounting book.

Compare these Custom House officials, if you will, with the Puritans in the opening chapters of *The Scarlet Letter*. These early inhabitants of Salem enjoy a robustness and vitality their descendants have lost.

Grim the characters may be and forbidding, severe even to cruelty in their treatment of Hester Prynne. But they keep their sights not on receipts of purchase, but on the eternal truths revealed to them by God.

The Puritans have belief, conviction, faith—choose whatever word you like to convey that inner force which makes a human being stand for something larger than himself. Perhaps you will say the Puritans have soul, if you mean by that an inviolate spirit.

CHAPTER 1: THE PRISON-DOOR

Hawthorne opens *The Scarlet Letter* just outside the prison of what, in the early 1640s, was the village of Boston.

Ask yourself what you know about a novel that begins in a prison. You probably suspect you are reading the story of a crime already committed, of characters whose lives are already darkened by guilt and disgrace. And, in the case of *The Scarlet Letter*, you are quite right.

Look carefully at the details of the opening scene: "The sad-colored garments" of the spectators; the prison-door itself, "heavily timbered with oak and studded with iron spikes." These details create a somber mood; they paint a cheerless picture. And they hint, as well, at a society that places punishment far above forgiveness on its scale of values.

One note of color relieves the gloom. A wild rose bush blossoms by the prison door. A natural thing, the rose bush suggests a world beyond the narrow confines of the Puritan community, where beauty and vibrant color flourish and crime finds tolerance and pity.

You will not know it yet. But even this early, Hawthorne has marked the thematic boundaries of his novel: law and nature, repression and freedom. In the following chapters, his characters will move back and forth between them.

CHAPTER 2: THE MARKET-PLACE

You will find much of *The Scarlet Letter* descriptive and analytical. But not the central scenes. These are dramatic enough to take your breath away.

"The Market-Place," for instance, is some curtain-raiser. In one vivid image, you have the whole story. The lines of conflict are drawn, the issues defined, the characters placed in relation to one another.

The image Hawthorne gives us is that of a young woman taken in adultery, and standing on a scaffold in the midst of a hostile crowd. (Wait a minute. An adulteress on display in the market-place? Yes. This is Puritan Boston, where private wrongdoing *is* public business.)

The woman has been brought to the scaffold for an ordeal of shaming, an ordeal she endures with stubborn pride. She does not drop her gaze, but instead responds to the angry stares of the crowd with quiet defiance.

In her arms, the woman carries an infant, one emblem of her sin. And on her breast, she wears another: a scarlet letter *A* (for Adulteress), intended by the magistrates to be a badge of shame, but already the subject of curious speculation.

On a nearby balcony, seated in a place of honor among the judges, is the woman's lover, the man who is supposed to be standing on the scaffold by her side. And on the outskirts of the crowd an interested observer, the woman's secret husband, watches, his keen eyes searching for his rival, his thoughts already turned to revenge.

It is a scene fraught with tension, brimming with possibilities. Let's explore some of them further.

In this first encounter in the market-place, the young woman, Hester Prynne, and the Puritan community are in fierce if silent conflict. They take the measures of one another. They bring into play opposing values.

On the one side is a woman who has violated a strict social and religious code, but who has sinned (if indeed, she has sinned) in an affirmation of love and life. On the other side is a grim and forbidding crowd which seems, nonetheless, to possess a certain degree of dignity and authority.

You will have to determine which side claims your sympathy—and Hawthorne's. The choice is not as cut-and-dried as it seems.

Let's take a closer look at the Puritan spectators waiting by the scaffold with such apparent eagerness to condemn one of their number. The severe expression on their faces, Hawthorne tells us, would be better suited to greet an infamous murderer (a Jack the Ripper, say) than an adulteress. He quickly adds, however, that this stern and unbending crowd would glower just as fiercely at a mischievous child brought before the magistrates for whipping.

We quickly sense in these Puritans a lack not only of sympathy but of discrimination. In their eyes, all crimes are equally reprehensible. And all criminals are to be treated with the full rigor of the law.

What about mercy? we wonder. What about that injunction not to cast the first stone? Not for this crowd. They can be downright bloodthirsty, especially the women. One hard-faced matron suggests branding Hester Prynne's forehead with a hot iron as a more appropriate punishment than the wearing of the scarlet letter. And a second woman goes further, calling for the death penalty.

It is tempting, when we hear such talk, to dismiss these Puritans as hard-hearted fanatics, to sense beneath their severity a strain of bigotry, and to cheerfully consign them to the hell they so fervently believed in.

It is tempting, but it is probably premature.

If we read this chapter carefully, we will see a more measured assessment on Hawthorne's part. Time and again, we find the author treating the Puritans like a coin of doubtful value that he turns over and over in his hand. If one side of the coin comes up dross, the other has gleams of real gold.

Let us turn now to the subject of all this unflattering attention, to Hester Prynne herself. She makes a striking contrast to the grim, joyless crowd of spectators. She walks into their midst with a radiance undimmed by her stay in prison. She carries herself with a stately, natural grace.

Hester is beautiful, of course. And her rich, deep complexion and her glossy black hair suggest a sensuality that—given the occasion—must have struck the self-righteous bystanders as a slap in the face.

Her first gesture on leaving the prison shows extraordinary dignity. Repelling the arm of the beadle (a minor town official), Hester steps of her own free will into the open air. It is the move of a woman who, even in the hands of the law, chooses to be seen in control of her own destiny.

Under the pressure of the moment, a lesser woman might have burst into tears or appealed for mercy, welcome signs to the magistrates, at least, of a lost sheep eager to return to the fold. But all these Puritan worthies get from Hester Prynne is a "burning blush," together with a haughty smile and a glance that refuses to falter in shame.

Hester does not speak. To get at her in this crucial moment of her life, we have to read the signs: her expression, where pride predominates in a mixture of emotions; her clothing, rich beyond the allowance of the colony's laws; and the scarlet letter, sewn by Hester in prison and worn this day by order of the Governor and the ministers.

And what a letter it is! Made not out of simple red flannel used for colds and rheumatism, as one irate woman observes, but elaborately embroidered with threads of gold. A badge of shame that looks more like a sign of defiance, thrown in the magistrates' teeth.

What are we to make of that letter? And its wearer, with her beauty, her daring, and her pride? Is Hester magnificent, a woman bravely standing up to unwarranted punishment? Or is she outrageous, flaunting her shame in the community's face?

Whatever she is, she is extraordinary, as she stands there on the scaffold, the focus of all eyes. And we are compelled to wonder what has brought her to this pass. Hawthorne obliges us with a few precious clues about Hester's past.

She is the daughter of impoverished English gentry, wed as a girl to an old, misshapen scholar who spent his days poring over dusty books. Sent on ahead of her husband to the New World, she found herself neither widow nor wife in a rugged frontier community where a woman alone had no place and no life. When we first encounter Hester, she has spent two years waiting for a man who may never come, a man whose arrival, in any case, cannot be welcome to her.

CHAPTER 3: THE RECOGNITION

As Hester Prynne stands on the scaffold, thinking of her husband, he appears before her startled eyes at the edge of the crowd. And his first gesture is indicative of the man. Whatever shock or dismay he may feel at seeing his wife on the scaffold, the object of public reproof, another man's child in her arms, he immediately suppresses his emotions and makes his face the image of calm.

By the time Hester's eyes meet his own, he has plotted his course of action. His plans demand secrecy. He indicates as much, and no more, to his wife by raising a finger to his lips.

What kind of man is this who can face the desecration of his home, the stain on his own honor (the 17th century was not kind to the men it called cuckolds) with hardly a raised eyebrow? Hawthorne gives us some clues in Chillingworth's face.

The glance he bends on Hester Prynne is keen and penetrative. Here is someone used to observing life rather than participating in it. His is a "furrowed visage," a face lined with years of thought and study by dim candle light. Chillingworth looks like a man who has cultivated his mind at the expense of all other faculties—a perilous enterprise, in Hawthorne's view. Where his overbearing intellect will take him, we will see in later chapters.

Chillingworth's finger raised to his lips, commanding Hester's silence, begins a pattern of secrecy that is the mainspring of the novel's plot.

Even as we meet Chillingworth, he goes underground. He assumes total ignorance of Hester and her situation. He takes on a new identity, that of a recently arrived physician, seeking the shelter of civilization after a stay among the savages.

As Chillingworth's conversation with the towns-man indicates, he will use his new position to solve the mystery that confronts him: the identity of his wife's lover. (Hawthorne did not know the word, but perhaps he would not object to our thinking of Chill-ingworth, in the language of modern espionage nov-els, as a "mole," or long-term secret agent.)

We now have *two* characters in hiding, a concealed husband and a concealed lover, the one gone into hid-ing to ferret out the other. We are hearing a lot of proud talk in this marketplace about the godly colony of Massachusetts, where "iniquity is dragged out into the sunshine." But we should note that, so far, some-thing pretty sinister is doing a good job of keeping itself under wraps.

The magistrates now address this question of hid-den evil in their own fashion. Turning to Hester Prynne, they attempt to prevail upon her to reveal the name of her partner in sin.

In a ringing voice that echoes through the crowd, the Reverend John Wilson, religious head of the col-ony, calls upon the adulteress to forego her "hardness and obstinacy" and identify the man who led her into error. But encountering only silence, Wilson admits defeat. He turns to Arthur Dimmesdale to second his apppeal.

NOTE: Wilson's urging of Hester Prynne is not merely investigative police work. In the Puritan scheme of things, Hester is a lost soul whose only hope of salvation lies in sincere and thorough repen-tance. Confession, in Wilson's own words, would be the "proof" of repentance, and the "consequence thereof." If Hester were truly sorry for her fault, she would not hesitate to put her lover, along with her-self, on the path of open contrition.

Well, it is a sticky moral point, this business of naming names. The great Salem witch hunt was shortly to come, when men and women would be asked to prove the pristine cleanliness of their souls by soiling the reputations of their friends and loved ones. In later chapters, Hawthorne will skirt the issue, sensibly enough, by putting the onus of confession where it belongs. It is not up to Hester Prynne to name her lover; the man should come forward himself.

Wilson's words turn our attention to Arthur Dimmesdale, seated on the balcony with the magistrates, but somehow apart from the rest. Dimmesdale is younger than the men who surround him, and softer. Against the icy sternness of the Puritan elders, he appears, if anything, too sensitive. There is a frightened look about the eyes, a certain trembling of the mouth.

The magistrates, we note, are men of action. Dimmesdale is a scholar, fresh from the great English universities. He is not at home in the marketplace. He prefers the seclusion of his study. Right now, he would give a lot to be at home with his books.

The minister seems to be frankly troubled to be witness to this spectacle at all. His presence has been required; it has not been a matter of choice. His intervention in the proceedings is also involuntary. He speaks to Hester Prynne only at Wilson's insistence.

Dimmesdale's appeal to Hester is quieter than Wilson's and far less self-assured. His call for confession is conditional; it leaves some freedom of choice. "*If* thou feelest it to be for thy soul's peace," he tells Hester, "I charge thee to speak out the name of thy fellow sinner."

Dimmesdale's arguments are also more personal than Wilson's, presumably closer to the heart of a woman in love. He urges Hester to confess for her lover's own good. She should not be silent out of misguided pity or affection. "Take heed how thou deniest to him—who, perchance, hath not the courage to grasp it for himself—the bitter, but wholesome, cup that is now presented to thy lips."

It is a moving appeal, a compelling line of reasoning, and a totally amazing speech, once we realize that Dimmesdale is talking against himself.

Every word the minister utters is charged with double meaning. Each inflection of his voice has one significance for the crowd of spectators, another for Hester Prynne who alone knows that Dimmesdale himself is the man the magistrates so urgently seek.

Dimmesdale is in a tight corner, one of the tightest in which a man of the cloth can find himself. He is a public official, under orders to elicit Hester's confession. He is also the private lover who benefits from her silence. As Hester's pastor, Dimmesdale has a moral obligation to seek the salvation of her soul. But as a man with a lot to lose, his interests lie in her continued resistance to religious authority.

Do you think Dimmesdale is sincere—or self-serving—in this plea he makes to Hester Prynne? It isn't easy to decide. Part of Dimmesdale seems truly to envy Hester the comparative luck of an open shame. But the deadly irony of his position takes much of the force and fire from his words.

Hester—either in accordance with or in opposition to her lover's real wishes—maintains her silence. Her refusal to speak gives us an opportunity to measure her generosity of spirit.

Another woman, exhibited for hours on the scaffold and left alone to bear the burden of public shame, might have decided, humanly enough, that two could bear the burden better than one. But Hester lifts the entire load onto her own strong shoulders. Looking straight into Dimmesdale's troubled eyes, she says, "Would that I might endure his agony as well as my own."

Dimmesdale, who should know, takes her silence for love. But we may sense, as well, an element of scorn in Hester's defiance of her judges. Wilson, who should have read her character better, makes her an offer that is little short of a bribe. If she names her lover to the authorities, they will consider a reversal of sentence. Confession may remove the scarlet letter from her breast.

Hester has understood, better than the magistrates, the meaning of the badge of shame they have forced upon her. For the first time (but not the last) in the novel, she claims the letter for her own, clutching it to herself with a mixture of pride and despair. "Never!" she answers Wilson, "The letter is too deeply branded. Ye cannot take it off."

She will forget that truth only once in her life, at an enormous cost.

CHAPTER 4: THE INTERVIEW

"The Interview" brings together the estranged husband and wife in the comparative privacy of the Boston prison. Chillingworth has come to the prison in his role of physician, sent for by the jailor who can no longer control his overwrought charges, Hester and Pearl. (Chillingworth, as we shall see, always manages to be sent for. It is part and parcel of his cleverness never to simply arrive.)

When Hester sees Chillingworth, she becomes as still as death. Her heart leaps into her throat. Hester has steeled herself to bear the day's trials, but her husband's unlooked-for arrival throws her completely off base.

Hester's bravado, which carried her through the ordeal in the market-place, deserts her now. She can barely look Chillingworth in the face. She feels all the shame and terror she never felt before the magistrates. This man has a right to punish her, perhaps even to take her life.

Hester, in fact, believes that Chillingworth has come to the prison with murder in his heart. When the physician hands her a draught of medicine to calm her down, Hester visibly hesitates, wondering if there is poison in the cup.

Poison? Don't be silly, Chillingworth replies. He adds that, if he wanted revenge, there were better, subtler ways than poison. After all, Chillingworth asks Hester, when have his purposes ever been "so shallow"?

Kind actions. Deep and subtle purposes. There is apparently a big difference between what Chillingworth does and what he means. What he does in this scene is just what we would expect of a skilled and kindly physician. He soothes Hester and her child with calming potions, quite possibly saving the infant's life. (In doing so, Chillingworth accomplishes what no other man in Boston is equipped to do. He has come to the prison with Sagamore remedies, medicines he has forced the New World to yield to his inquiring mind.)

And Chillingworth goes beyond the relief of physical suffering. For one brief moment, he offers Hester a fair measure of understanding. The ill-used husband takes on himself a share of the blame for his wife's downfall. "It was my folly, and thy weakness. I,—a man of thought,—the bookworm of great libraries,—a man already in decay,—what had I to do with youth and beauty like thine own!"

Yes, it was folly, especially in a scholar like himself. Surely he had read enough about December-May marriages to have foreseen the disastrous ending of his own. Men called him wise, but wise he clearly was not. And here they both were, with this grievous mess on their hands.

What have we here? A self-aware human being? A man, among all these self-righteous Puritans, capable of seeing life not in black and white but in various shades of gray. It is a fascinating glimpse of a character that might have been, a Chillingworth who might have commanded our respect, if not our sympathy.

But it is only a glimpse, and then Hawthorne shuts the door. We are left, instead, with a villainous thing whose fingers scorch Hester's flesh as they brush the scarlet letter, and whose glowing eyes threaten to read the secrets of her innermost soul.

All this demonic imagery is a sign of evil intent, for Chillingworth's real purpose is coming to the fore. He is planning revenge, though not against Hester. It is her lover he seeks. Chillingworth has come to the prison to ask the man's name. Does Hester refuse it? No matter. The man shall be his in any case. His for some unspeakable form of revenge: not murder, not dishonor, something worse.

Somewhere along the line, Chillingworth has crossed a boundary. He is not in the human realm any more, but in the demonic sphere of soul possession. Hester senses it. She says, underscoring the split in Chillingworth we have felt all along. "Thy acts are like mercy, but thy words interpret thee as a terror!"

A terror he is indeed. Why then does Hester promise Chillingworth the shield of her silence? Perhaps guilt comes into play. Chillingworth is asking to be spared the dishonor of a cuckold, and Hester feels she owes him at least this much. Perhaps fatigue also plays a part. Hester is no match for Chillingworth after the turmoils of the day.

But Hester's main motive is to spare her lover the scaffold. She has no doubt that Chillingworth will ferret him out. And Chillingworth has threatened, should Hester reveal his secret, that her lover's name and reputation will be forfeit.

"I will keep thy secret, as I have his," Hester swears to Chillingworth.

Nonetheless, Hester has qualms. Having given her word, she wonders if she has been lured into a pact with the devil that will prove the ruination of her soul.

"Not *thy* soul," Chillingworth answers, implying that another soul than Hester's will be damned. Chillingworth means the soul of Hester's lover, but, as we shall see, it turns out to be his own.

CHAPTER 5: HESTER AT HER NEEDLE

For Hester's violation of the Puritan code, the magistrates inflict two punishments: first, the hours of shame on the scaffold; and second, the life-long burden of the scarlet letter.

In this chapter, Hawthorne turns to the long, gray years following the turbulent scene in the marketplace. Do the years show us a different Hester Prynne?

Many readers of *The Scarlet Letter* see the start of a great change in Hester, a move away from the fierce defiance of the opening chapters towards a growing acceptance of her fate. As evidence of a new softness and contrition, they point to:

1. Hester's Decision to Remain in Puritan Boston She might, Hawthorne tells us, have left the narrow-minded colony to start life all over again in a place where no one knew her story. The sea leads back to England or, for a woman of Hester's strength, the track leads onward into the wilderness. But Hester turns her back on these escape routes. She stays in the settlement, shackled, as if by an iron chain of guilt, to the scene of her crime and punishment.

2. Hester's Sedate Appearance Hester has changed the rich clothing of the scaffold scene for a modest, nondescript dress. In her rejection of finery, she is more severe than her Puritan neighbors, who employ Hester's needle for such occasional luxuries as christening robes and gorgeously embroidered gloves.

3. Hester's Charity to the Poor Hester uses her spare hours not for the detailed work she loves, but in the making of coarse garments for the colony's indigent. It is an act of penance for which she gets small thanks. The poor receive her gifts with insults.

Hester now moves quietly and usefully through the community, bowing her head as indignities are heaped upon it. Have we a newly chastened woman? Some readers think so. Yet others question just how deeply Hester has been stained with the Puritan dye and imbued with the Puritans' somber vision of life. They see hints of the old fire, that inflammable mixture of passion, recklessness, and despair. They argue:

1. Hester has chosen to stay in the Puritan settlement for a reason she dares not admit, even to herself: the man she loves is there. Here is the tie she feels to Boston, an unblessed union to be recognized in the next world, if not in this one.

2. Hester subdues her taste for the beautiful out of a guilty conscience. She knows all is not well with herself, so she has come to reject as sin all that she finds natural or pleasurable. The sewing of beautiful things would be innocent enough outlet for the sensuous streak in her nature. But she denies herself innocent outlets, only to bottle up feelings that will one day explode.

3. Hester's acts of charity are a camouflage for anger and bitterness. Though she sews for the poor, she wishes them to the devil. She may show outward patience when insulted and abused, but inwardly she is stung to the quick.

NOTE: With her consummate skill as a seamstress and her taste for the gorgeously beautiful, Hester is an artist. Or the nearest thing to an artist that Puritan New England allows. In this capacity, at least, she has Hawthorne's full sympathy. An artist himself, Hawthorne has suffered imaginary, but painful, reprimands from his Puritan forebears. He knows, and wrestles, with the fact that his work is at best trivial, at worst dangerous, in their eyes. (See "The Custom House.")

Perhaps we can sense a struggle in Hester Prynne to define her new relations with the society she has offended. Once she engaged the Puritan world in head-to-head combat. Now the conflict has moved within herself.

We can learn a lot from Hester's choice of a home. She moves into a small cottage on the outskirts of town. She lives not within shouting distance of her neighbors, but still within the boundaries that define the settlement.

It is a narrow foothold that Hester maintains in a community that offers her no support or human warmth, but that does not entirely cast her off.

CHAPTER 6: PEARL

This chapter introduces us to the most problematic character in *The Scarlet Letter*. Pearl is half child, half literary symbol. And to many readers, she is no child at all.

You will have to decide for yourself how successful Pearl is as a literary creation. Does she seem to you a living, breathing being, or a cardboard figure, stiff and unreal?

One thing is certain. In appearance and temperament Pearl reflects her origin. The product of a broken rule, she will not obey rules herself. Born of a runaway passion, she has a wild and stormy nature.

Pearl's high coloring and warm complexion are the gifts of her mother. They also suggest the fiery state of Hester's emotions during her term of imprisonment.

To some extent, Pearl reflects the common folk wisdom that love-children are more beautiful and more passionate than the issue of a stale marriage bed. But the matter goes deeper than that.

Pearl's uncontrolled rages at her Puritan peers—priggish little brats that they are—and the hostile playmates she invents with her fertile imagination, express her sense of alienation, her recognition that she is an outcast's child.

With her outbursts of temper, Pearl is a constant reproach to Hester for bringing an innocent being into an adverse world. She is a reminder of the far-reaching, unthought-of consequences of sin. But nothing that Pearl does causes Hester so much anguish as the child's uncanny fascination with the scarlet letter.

The letter is the first object of Pearl's consciousness. As her infant hands reach for the threads of red and gold her face takes on a knowing smile, "a decided gleam." The letter is the subject of her play. She makes it a target for a barrage of flowers which she hurls at her mother, jumping up and down with glee, each time a missile hits home.

Does Pearl understand what she is doing? Does she realize what the letter means? Hawthorne doesn't say, though Hester half humorously, half desparingly, credits her child with preternatural (more than natural) intelligence.

The effect of Pearl's behavior, whatever the cause, is to keep Hester's sense of shame fresh and acute. The wound is not allowed to heal. Even in the privacy of her cottage, away from the prying eyes of the community, Hester is not for a moment safe.

NOTE: There are many suggestions in this chapter and the following ones, that Pearl is not a human child. Her light, eerie laughter reminds Hester of an elf. At times, an imp or a demon looks out of Pearl's eyes. Governor Bellingham will say that the child has witchcraft in her. And some people in the colony call Pearl the devil's offspring.

This method of characterization, by multiple suggestions, is used often in the novel. But Hawthorne is up to something rather special in Pearl's case.

He wants to take Pearl out of the ordinary human realm—the dark Puritan world of guilt and sorrow—and present the child to us against the rich and colorful backdrop of nature.

CHAPTER 7: THE GOVERNOR'S HALL

"The Governor's Hall" contains one of the most detailed and fully realized settings in *The Scarlet Letter*. To write it, Hawthorne had to do his homework, indepth historical research.

There really was a Governor Bellingham in mid–17th-century Boston. Hawthorne found an accurate description of his home in one of the most creditable books on the period, Snow's *History of Boston*.

What Snow gave Hawthorne was an altogether prosaic description of a wooden house covered with plaster. The plaster was dotted with bits of broken glass from common junk bottles. There were also drawings on it of squares, diamonds, and fleur-de-lis.

If you turn to Hawthorne's description in paragraph nine, you may get some clues as to how his creative imagination works. (The paragraph begins, "Without further adventure, they reached the dwelling of Governor Bellingham.")

Hawthorne has taken the house he found in Snow, and he's romanced it. The broken junk bottles have become fistfuls of diamonds. The humdrum tracings in the plaster are now cabalistic (secret and mystic) messages. Instead of a local relic, we have a palace from *Arabian Nights*.

The hint of oriental magnificence is admittedly playful. More serious, is the double historical perspective from which Hawthorne observes the house. He stands with one foot in the 17th, one foot in the 19th, century.

He describes the house first, as if it were right there before him, a 200-year-old mansion. And then he imaginatively strips it of the accretions of time—the moss, the dust, the emotional residue of lives—to show us the house as it was in 1640, sparkling, clean, and new.

Inside the mansion, the *Chronicles of England* lies open on the window seat, as if someone has been called away in the middle of a page. A large pewter tankard has a foamy bit of ale in it, as if someone has just taken a draught and put it down. A suit of armor, fresh from the London armorer, stands polished and ready for use, not for show.

The whole effect is like walking into the preserved home of a famous historical figure and watching what we thought was a museum spring magically to life.

NOTE: The armor in Bellingham's hall has a second purpose. It is a distorted mirror that magnifies the scarlet letter on Hester's dress and diminishes the woman who wears it. Here, in the Governor's mansion, at the heart of the Puritan establishment, Hester Prynne, the individual, vanishes behind the symbol of her shame.

Hester has come to Bellingham's home, disturbed by rumors of a movement afoot to take Pearl away from her. The leaders of the community, the Governor chief among them, have decided that the child's welfare would be better served if she were placed in worthier hands.

Hester arrives determined to fight for her rights as a mother. But the outfit in which she has clothed Pearl is a doubtful argument in her favor.

Pearl wears a crimson velvet tunic, embroidered with gold. It is, to put it mildly, an outlandish costume in a society where black and gray are the going colors. Bellingham will find in the child's outfit all the more reason to place Pearl in a home where she will be "soberly clad."

Why has Hester dressed her daughter so peculiarly? Just in case we miss the point, Hawthorne makes it explicit. Pearl is the scarlet letter "come to life." Hester has lavished all her skill as a seamstress on a dress that points out the likeness between the two emblems of her sin.

CHAPTER 8: THE ELF-CHILD AND THE MINISTER

We come, in this chapter, to a second contest between Hester Prynne and the magistrates, this time over Pearl. Hester is so strong in her sense of natural right—the right of a mother to her child—that she seems almost a match for these stern and rigorous law makers. Almost.

At the first sight of Pearl, the magistrates gathered in the Governor's hall are taken aback. They don't know what to make of the high-spirited child. In her red velvet tunic, Pearl seems to them like an apparition from another—and an older and gayer—world.

She reminds Wilson of the glowing reflections cast by the stained glass windows of the high Gothic cathedrals in Europe. And she recalls to Bellingham the unruly children of the English court theatricals. (Neither association is flattering. The Puritans in England wrecked the ornate churches and closed down the theatres in the belief that luxuriant art and bawdy drama alike corrupt the soul.)

The old men are kindly to Pearl, but clearly disapproving. When the child fails to recite her catechism properly, they consider the question of Hester's continued custody to be closed. Pearl will be taken from her mother.

NOTE: When Reverend Wilson asks Pearl, "Who made thee?" the child replies that she was plucked by her mother off the wild rosebush that grows by the prison door.

Though Hawthorne suggests a realistic explanation for Pearl's answer (her response was triggered by the red roses in the Governor's garden), he clearly wants us to perceive a kinship between Pearl and a wild thing in nature. Like the rosebush, Pearl is exempt from rules and regulations. She flourishes outside the realm of human law.

Bellingham and Wilson are understandably shocked by Pearl's reply, which shows an apparent lack of religious training. But they are somewhat less shocked than they would be if they could read its full meaning (the full extent, that is, of Pearl's claim to freedom).

In their decision to put Pearl in a proper, God-fearing home, the Governor and Wilson have not reckoned with Hester Prynne. The mother is prepared to fight like a lioness for her cub. Clutching Pearl tightly in her arms, Hester cries out her defiance. They shall not take Pearl from her. She will die first.

Hester's entreaties, however, fall on deaf ears. She turns in desperation to her one possible source of help. She has spied, in Arthur Dimmesdale, a potential ally in the enemy camp.

Hester has sensed Dimmesdale's presence all along, though she has not acknowledged it until now. Probably she would leave him out of the quarrel, if she could. (She has never cashed in on their former intimacy to ask the minister for favors.) But she cannot afford that luxury at the moment. Having little choice, she turns to the clergyman with a "wild and singular" appeal. It is, in fact, less an appeal than an ultimatum.

> 'Speak for me! Thou knowest—for thou hast sympathies which these men lack—thou knowest what is in my heart, and what are a mother's rights, and how much the stronger they are, when that mother has but her child and the scarlet letter! Look thou to it! I will not lose the child! Look to it![1]

Here is the second private exchange between Hester Prynne and Arthur Dimmesdale that has taken place in full view of an uncomprehending audience. Hester is addressing Dimmesdale, of course, not as her pastor, but as the unnamed father of her child.

Although she does not explicitly threaten to give Dimmesdale away, the implication is there. Don't drive me too far, she is saying, or who knows what I'll do. Her words remind the minister of the sacrifice she has made to keep him in a position of influence. He had better use that influence to help her now.

(Is this the same Hester Prynne who promised Dimmesdale her silence from the scaffold and who has protected him from exposure for so long? The fact that Hester is willing to threaten the minister now suggests that nothing—not her pride or her generosity—matter to her as much as Pearl.)

Dimmesdale, honestly moved by Hester's distress and perhaps just as honestly frightened by her implied threats, comes forward to intervene on her behalf.

Dimmesdale succeeds in swaying Bellingham and Wilson where Hester has failed. In part, he uses Hester's arguments and lends them—suspect as they are in her mouth—the force of his moral authority. He speaks of the solemn miracle of Pearl's existence. The child, he says, is a gift from God, meant for a blessing and retribution, too. Because Hester loves Pearl so dearly, he implies, the child can touch her mother's heart with an agony far more exquisite than any inflicted by the scarlet letter. (Pearl is doing the job you wanted done, he might almost have told them. Let it be.)

So much Hester has said herself. But Dimmesdale sees further. He recognizes that Pearl is Hester's one remaining link with humanity, a responsibility that will save her from the reckless actions to which she might be tempted as an outcast from society.

Dimmesdale's belief is quickly vindicated by a strange interview between Hester and Mistress Hibbins, the Governor's sister, a woman suspected by Puritan Boston (and herself) of being a witch. Mistress Hibbins invites Hester to dance in the forest that night. And Hester declines, saying she must stay at home and watch over Pearl.

CHAPTER 9: THE LEECH

If you look up the word *leech* in the dictionary, you will find the meaning you expect: a blood-sucking insect. But you will also find an archaic meaning, that of physician. In past centuries doctors were known as leeches because of their common practice of bleeding patients. (It was thought to rid the body of bad humors.)

The title of this chapter is characteristically ambiguous. It points, on the one hand, to Chillingworth's newly assumed career as a doctor, and, on the other hand, to his role as emotional parasite. He is now a man who lives off another's suffering. Like Chillingworth himself, the title has a surface meaning as well as a deeper one.

Let's look at the surface meaning for a moment. As a doctor, Chillingworth is entirely convincing. His professional manners are impeccable. He does not seek Dimmesdale out aggressively. He approaches the clergyman by way of the upper echelons of the ministry, leaving it to what we would call the church's board of directors to recommend his services.

Chillingworth is courteous and self-effacing. His overtures to his reluctant patient are low-key. When Dimmesdale, denying his need for a doctor's care, says that he would be well content to die if it were God's will, Chillingworth is quick to attribute to the minister only the best, and least personal, of motives. " 'Ah . . . it is thus that a young clergyman is apt to speak . . . saintly men, who walk with God on earth, would fain be away, to walk with Him on the golden pavements of the New Jerusalem.' "

Such comments are ingenious. They reflect the community's reverence for Dimmesdale, and so keep the minister off guard. But they also offer just that hint of overpiety that cuts the grounds for objecting to medical care from under Dimmesdale's feet. (If Dimmesdale is in such a hurry to die, Chillingworth is suggesting, he must be awfully sure of a place in a better world.)

By such careful handling of Dimmesdale, Chillingworth maneuvers himself into the position of intimate friend and constant attendant. He becomes a sounding board for the minister's ideas, a recipient of confidences—medical and otherwise. He hears Dimmesdale's thoughts as they pass all but uncensored from his lips.

NOTE: We can learn a lot from Dimmesdale's initial reaction to Chillingworth. The minister is, at first, fascinated by the breadth of the physician's mind. Though orthodox himself, Dimmesdale has a sneaking fondness for radical ideas in others. In the stuffy intellectual atmosphere of Boston, he has had no such stimulation for a long time. Perhaps we can see what originally attracted him to Hester Prynne. Here was one woman, among a hundred dull and strait-laced girls, who dared to think for herself.

If you think you spy in Chillingworth the familiar outline of a modern psychiatrist, you are perceptive— and half right. There was no science of psychiatry in Hawthorne's day, but Chillingworth casts on the wall the shadow of things to come.

Hawthorne knew what could happen if a doctor attuned his mind to a patient's, listened quietly to his revelations, registered no shock or surprise at his thoughts, however monstrous. He knew, and he found such cold scrutiny repulsive.

Perhaps a benign motive on the physician's part would redeem such investigative procedures. But Chillingworth's motives, as we know, are entirely malevolent.

Chillingworth is guilty of more than a betrayal of friendship or an abuse of a doctor's privilege. He is trespassing on holy ground, entering with irreverent curiosity the sacred precincts of another man's soul.

He is also shoveling away all of Dimmesdale's virtues to find the lode of evil he suspects. And while he is digging, he begins to show signs of getting dirty. Rumors are rife in Boston. Popular opinion, which first proclaimed the doctor's arrival a miracle, now has taken a different turn. The fires in Chillingworth's laboratory are said to be fed with infernal fuel, and his face is getting dark and grimy from the smoke.

You can accept popular opinion. You can view Chillingworth as an arch villain or even a fiend. But you also see him as something more interesting than that: a man playing a deadly game with his enemy, deadly in a way he does not even suspect.

Chillingworth, after all, has made his own life dependent on Dimmesdale's. Revenge is his sole reason to exist. As the title of the chapter reminds us, a leech is a parasite that dies along with its host.

CHAPTER 10: THE LEECH AND HIS PATIENT

Hawthorne portrays the relationship between Chillingworth and Dimmesdale with such intensity, we tend to forget that it covers a span of years. Chillingworth has worked with silent caution, consolidating his position as Dimmesdale's friend and counselor. The doctor now shares the minister's quarters, the better to keep his patient under his wing.

Perhaps Chillingworth feels sure enough of his position to take some calculated risks. We come upon him now as he broaches a dangerous and volatile topic: hidden sin.

The doctor has come in with an ugly weed plucked from a nearby graveyard. He tells Dimmesdale that the weed represents some guilty secret that was buried with the corpse.

Dimmesdale takes the bait. In his experience, the minister says, men find great comfort in confession. Undoubtedly, the dead man longed to tell his secret, but could not do so.

The discussion is, on the surface, remote, theoretical. But we read it with the same feeling of suspense we would experience if we were watching the two men wrestle at the edge of a cliff. Will one of them, we wonder, lose his balance and fall?

Dimmesdale, with less control, is in graver danger. As Chillingworth intends, the discussion is getting to him. The minister begins to talk, not about men in general, but about himself. He offers a justification for silence that lies close to his heart.

Perhaps men shrink from confession, Dimmesdale says, because once they have sullied their reputations, they no longer have a hope of redeeming past evil with future good deeds. Confessed sinners put themselves beyond the pale of society, where they can no longer serve God or their fellow men.

What do you think of Dimmesdale's argument? Is there truth in what he says? Are good intentions a valid reason for presenting a fale face to the world?

Chillingworth dismisses Dimmesdale's reasoning as pure rationalization. Such men deceive themselves, the physician replies. If they wish to serve others, let them do so by showing the power of conscience in their own lives. " 'Wouldst thou have me to believe, O wise and pious friend, that a false show can be better—can be more for God's glory, or man's welfare—than God's own truth?' "

Here is the other side of the argument, neatly phrased and incisively put. A lie is never good, and never leads to good. Do you find Chillingworth's argument more convincing than Dimmesdale's? Perhaps the minister does, too. And yet, Chillingworth remains unmoved by his own words. He is uttering these pious truths only to play on Dimmesdale's guilt.

It bothers Chillingworth not one iota that he, as much as Dimmesdale, is living a lie.

NOTE: The question of just how to take Chillingworth's statements is one we shall encounter often in the novel. The man is evil and insidious, yet his words often have the pure, crystal ring of truth. Are we to trust Chillingworth's judgments, even though we distrust the man? Or to put it another way, are we to take scripture on faith when the devil quotes it for his own use?

The tense discussion between Dimmesdale and Chillingworth is interrupted by the merry laughter of Pearl that comes floating in through the window. The child is up to her usual tricks. She is playing with the scarlet letter, outlining the red token on Hester's dress with burrs that prick less than her own cool indifference. The look of pain on Hester's face suggests to Chillingworth a question that directly relates to the topic under discussion. Is Hester the less miserable because her sin is known, her shame open?

Keep that question in mind. It will reoccur throughout *The Scarlet Letter*, with answers that vary from a firm yes to a tentative maybe. Dimmesdale now replies that Hester is comparatively lucky in the freedom she has to show her pain. (We remember he has said much the same thing in his speech to Hester in the market-place. To the minister, the grass always looks greener on Hester's side of the fence; that is, until he seriously considers joining her there.)

Chillingworth now turns to the subject of Dimmesdale's health. Has the minister revealed all the symptoms of his illness? The doctor has the physical signs well in hand. But are there spiritual disturbances as well, which he should be aware of?

The question touches a raw nerve in Dimmesdale. The storm breaks, one that has been brewing since the beginning of the scene. In a rage, Dimmesdale turns on Chillingworth. The doctor is out of his province. Earthly physicians have no business meddling with the ills of the soul.

The two men have reached a critical point in their relationship. For a moment, Dimmesdale has seen the malice in Chillingworth's eyes. He has recognized his enemy. But he backs down, filled with self-doubt.

Chillingworth, too, has had a glimpse of what lies beneath the veil. He has penetrated Dimmesdale's reserve and found the streak of passion he's always suspected in the man. And he finds something else.

Coming upon Dimmesdale in the deep sleep of exhaustion that follows this draining scene, Chillingworth thrusts aside a piece of cloth that, up to now, has always hidden the minister's chest from sight. And he sees—well, you know what he sees: a letter over the minister's heart that corresponds to the one on Hester's dress.

NOTE: In the closing image of Chillingworth— stamping his feet and throwing his arms toward the ceiling in joy and wonder at his discovery—we have an explicit comparison of the man to the fiend. We have come a long way, in a single chapter, from the upright man, "calm in temperament, kindly, though not of warm affections," to Satan, rejoicing in the damnation of a soul. To a large extent, this is the turning point in Hawthorne's protrayal of Chillingworth. The devil in him will be in the ascendant from here on.

CHAPTER 11: THE INTERIOR OF A HEART

We have been watching a split in Chillingworth between the inner and outer man. Now we turn to a similar division in Dimmesdale. This chapter explores the widening gap between the saintly minister perceived by the community and the abject sinner Dimmesdale knows himself to be.

The title of the chapter is important. The interior of a heart is where reality lies. It is a dark interior in these guilt-stricken characters of Hawthorne. The author leads us into the dim recesses of the minister's mind, as if he were entering a cavern, bearing a torch.

In the gloom, we find despair and self-loathing so extreme, the case borders on insanity. Dimmesdale is living a lie. Worse, he is living a lie in the sight of a God who knows and loves the truth. As a priest, Dimmesdale meant to guide his thoughts and actions by a higher, clearer light than other men. But here he is cowering in the dark, as if the dark could hide him.

Dimmesdale's agony is only intensified by the appalling irony of his situation. The worse he feels, the better he appears in the eyes of his congregation.

It's tough to deal with a reward you haven't earned, tough even if you aren't a Puritan with a tender conscience. Dimmesdale, remember, is not just a Puritan, he's a Puritan minister. And hypocrisy is not an occasional fault of his. It's become a way of life.

Dimmesdale grows pale and thin. Why, he's too pure to eat! His sermons take on a new and moving note. Ah, the people of Boston think, Heaven has chosen their minister for its mouthpiece. Dimmesdale even confesses from the pulpit. But his general avowal of sin is so much in line with Puritan orthodoxy (a conviction of sin was supposed to be the first step towards grace) that the impression of his purity is only heightened.

Dimmesdale is not even successful at lying to himself. He recognizes his vague confessions for the cheats that they are. His self-contempt only increases with every half-hearted attempt he makes to set himself right.

NOTE: The increasing power of Dimmesdale's sermons should perhaps be considered separately from the other effects of sin on his life. *The Scarlet Letter* is a book about the wages of sin, and the wages of sin can be surprising. In Dimmesdale's case, the immediate experience of guilt and sexuality have given this scholar-recluse the necessary common touch. He has come out of his ivory tower and down to earth. Sin has put him on a par with his parishioners. As a result, he can talk to them instead of *down to* them.

Dimmesdale now indulges in some morbid forms of penance. He takes up fasting and fasts until he faints. He takes a whip to his shoulders and beats himself until he bleeds.

Is this sheer masochism? Perhaps. Some readers believe the minister takes a perverse delight in self-torture. But there are other possible explanations for Dimmesdale's near-pathological behavior. To starve or scourge the sin from his soul would be an easier solution than tarnishing the bright image of himself which he sees reflected daily in the eyes of his congregants. And there is something else. The whips and fasts might give Dimmesdale the chance to feel something real again, even if what he feels is only real hunger and real pain.

Life for the minister has become increasingly shadowy. Lacking substance in himself, he finds substance in nothing. The world no longer gives him a handle to grasp. The very objects of his bedchamber—the heavy leather Bible, the thick oak table—have lost their heft and solidity. Dimmesdale begins to see through things, almost to walk through them, like a ghost.

CHAPTER 12: THE MINISTER'S VIGIL

This chapter brings Dimmesdale to the scaffold to stand where Hester Prynne has stood, in a frank and open declaration that he is the man who belonged by her side seven years before. A frank and open declaration, yes. But one made in the middle of the night, when no one can see.

Another incomplete act of penance! But Dimmesdale is getting closer now. The old fastings and scourgings took place in the privacy of his bedroom. This vigil is in the market-place, downtown Boston, so to speak. Someone might come along.

Someone does come along, quite a few people, in fact, given the lateness of the hour. The first person to pass unsuspectingly by is Reverend John Wilson, on his way home from Governor Winthrop's deathbed.

Seeing the gleam from Wilson's lantern, Dimmesdale is seized by a mad impulse to jest with the old clergyman. " 'Come up hither . . .' he nearly calls out, 'and pass a pleasant hour with me!' "

If Dimmesdale had spoken aloud, we can easily believe the sober, gray-haired Wilson would have dropped his lantern in astonishment, shocked as much by the uncharacteristic joke as by Dimmesdale's presence by the pillory.

And we are as surprised as Wilson would have been. We hardly know what to make of this lurid fit of playfulness, so much at odds with Dimmesdale's usual sad manner. Is the minister going mad at last? Or is this just a spell of gallows humor, the kind of mood that seizes people at moments of great danger and makes them laugh? We can't be sure yet. But we should note for future reference the unaccustomed energy that buoys Dimmesdale up when, as it seems, the devil is in him.

Meanwhile, more visitors intrude upon the minister's privacy. But this time, they are welcome. Hester and Pearl, also returning from Winthrop's bedside, mount the scaffold at Dimmesdale's pressing invitation.

The three figures, outlined against the night sky, make a dim, obscure picture, a shadow show of the real scene of confession which should take place in daylight. The shadow show is enough for Dimmesdale, giving him the first measure of peace he has known in years. (Like so many of us, the minister will settle for half-truths, where possible.) But it is not enough for Pearl.

Twice the child demands of the minister, will he take her hand and her mother's "tomorrow noontide"? On hearing Dimmesdale's reply—no, not in the light of this world—Pearl struggles to withdraw her hand from the minister's and run away.

NOTE: Once again, Pearl is operating on two levels. We can see her as a very normal child, an orphan whose persistent questions reflect a search for identity. Pearl has found a father or father-figure in Dimmesdale. And she resents what she correctly interprets as his rejection of her. A fleeting caress in the moonlight is not enough for Pearl. She wants to be acknowledged in broad daylight.

We can also see Pearl operating as a symbol, a flesh-and-blood counterpart to the scarlet letter. On this level, she has a mission to perform in Dimmesdale's life, just as she has in Hester's. She is a constant reminder to the minister of a deed not done, a truth not admitted.

Pearl's departure is halted by a meteor that floods the night sky with an unearthly light. The figures on the scaffold stand illuminated now, as if on the Day of Judgment—the minister with his hand over the *A* on his heart; Hester wearing her scarlet *A;* and Pearl, herself a symbol, between them—under a fiercely glowing A in the sky.

It is a perfect symbolic tableau, a set piece rather like medieval painting, where each of the figures has an allegorical meaning. It is a perfect symbolic tableau, that is, if there is an *A* in the sky at all. Dimmesdale has read the dull red lines of the letter in the meteor's trail, but "another's guilt might have seen another symbol in it."

What is Hawthorne up to? Why does he give us a symbol, ring all the changes on it, and then say he doesn't mean it? (Or only half means it. The sexton, we note, also sees an A in the sky, but he interprets the letter as a sign that Winthrop has become an angel.)

CHAPTER 13: ANOTHER VIEW OF HESTER

In many ways, "Another View of Hester" picks up where "Hester at Her Needle" left off. This second portrait of Hester presents us with many of the same questions as the first. How far has Hester traveled on the road to repentance? To what extent does she now accept the tenets of Puritan religion and law? Have all the years of suffering and good works brought about in Hester the change that the magistrates originally sought?

On the surface, Hester's submission to society has deepened. She lives more than ever in conformity with the rigid Puritan code. With no reputation to lose, Hester has conducted herself with such circumspection that not the busiest gossip in Boston can find a hint of scandal to report. Hester's charity to the poor continues, and she accepts, without complaint, the ill usage she receives at their hands.

What's more, Hester has taken new steps to redeem herself in the eyes of God and man. She has become a self-ordained Sister of Mercy. Her new role is that of tender and competent nurse to the colony's ill and dying.

The scarlet letter has become a sign of Hester's community with people in trouble. In households darkened by sorrow, the red token glimmers with comfort. A grateful, if fickle, public has invested the scarlet letter with a new meaning. The *A* no longer stands for "Adulteress." It now means "Able."

Had Hester been a Catholic, following the exposure of her guilty love she might have entered a cloister and taken the veil. In fact, she becomes the nearest thing to a nun that Protestant New England allows. She rejects love as firmly as she rejects all other worldly pleasures. In the crucible of fire through which she has passed, her sensuality seems burned away. With her austere dress and her demure cap that hides every strand of rich, luxuriant hair, Hester seems like a marble statue, unlikely as stone to seek or return an embrace.

It is a cold and joyless woman Hawthorne gives us in this chapter, a woman whose life has turned from feeling to thought. An innocent enough pasttime, you might suppose, compared with the seduction of saintly ministers? Not in Puritan Boston. Not on your life!

Condemned as an adulteress, Hester has become a free thinker, something far more dangerous in this stuffy, illiberal world. Once she was a dissenter, a person who broke with her society over a single law. Now she is a heretic, a person who questions the basis of *every* law.

In an earlier chapter of the novel, Hawthorne told us "The scaffold of the pillory was a point of view." And so it is. From that doubtful eminence, Hester has observed her society and found it wanting. She has always possessed a vision of a richer, warmer, freer existence than any permitted by the Puritans. And now, she is critical, too, of the dismal position that women hold in her world.

Are we to see Hester's intellectual independence as a good or bad thing? To quarrel with it goes against the American grain. Freedom of thought and conscience is the essence of our tradition. We are reluctant to deny anyone this first prerogative in life.

And yet, there is another side to the coin of free speculation. Someone like Hester, an outcast from society who lives on the edge of the wilderness, has no recourse to other minds and ideas, even in books. She has nothing to go on but her own rum experience, her admittedly distorted view of life. It is possible to argue that even the Puritan beliefs—stringent and mean as they are—have more validity than Hester's own. (Hawthorne will later say that shame, despair, and solitude have been Hester's teachers, and they have taught her "much amiss.")

NOTE: Once again, a cultural debate of the 19th century informs Hawthorne's fiction. Emerson and the optimists of his party believed in intellectual self-reliance to the exclusion of everything else. In their eyes, traditional religion was unnecessary, social conformity counter-productive. All a person needed to do was to listen attentively to the voice of his or her conscience.

Hawthorne's answer to Emerson, by way of Hester Prynne, was that the uninstructed voice of conscience could be misleading. We needed all the help we could get from religion, society, history, philosophy, and law. A mind in isolation ignored cultural truths at its peril—and could turn out to be dead wrong.

We should note that Hester's criticism of society ends in speculation and stops short of action. She never becomes a reformer or what we might call an advocate of women's liberation. Perhaps you will view Hester's silence as a failure of nerve. But to Hawthorne, it is clearly a saving grace. His view of women is conservative. He believes (wince, if you like) that a woman's proper province is the home and not the soapbox. Bad enough that Hester has become an intellectual. He will never make her an activist.

Male chauvinism aside, it is important to realize that we have in Hester yet another character with a gap between thought and feeling, a split between the inner and outer self. Hester's emotions are crushed, or buried deep within her. Her ideas in her society are literally unspeakable. As a result, Hester, like Dimmesdale and Chillingworth, is leading a double life.

CHAPTER 14: HESTER AND THE PHYSICIAN

The sight of Dimmesdale on the scaffold has given Hester a shock. She never knew the minister was so demoralized. She realizes now that, by her silence, she has left Dimmesdale far too long under Chillingworth's evil influence. She will seek out her husband to prevent what further damage she can.

Why has Hester never thought of speaking up before? Perhaps because she felt a bit resentful toward Dimmesdale. She has imagined him in a cozy position of honor and respect, while she was all the while suffering disgrace. She realizes now that she has misread the man. Clearly Dimmesdale has been suffering, too.

Before you go on with "Hester and the Physician," flip back to "The Interview," the earlier confrontation between Hester and Chillingworth. You will find that the balance of power has changed. The soft creature who could be manipulated by her husband is gone, replaced by a woman almost frightening in her strength.

If Hester has grown, Chillingworth has diminished. The years have shriveled him up. He stoops now when he walks, and his face has a dark, furtive look.

Hester, noting the change in her husband, is stricken with guilt. She believes Chillingworth's deterioration is, in part, traceable to herself.

NOTE: You will notice that Hester is willing to shoulder an enormous burden of responsibility. She feels guilty about Dimmesdale because she has left him, an unknowing victim, in Chillingworth's hands. And she feels guilty about Chillingworth because her betrayal of him has turned him into a nasty, vindictive man.

You will have to decide how much of this tragic situation is really Hester's fault, and how much of it is due to a weakness in Dimmesdale and a lack of mental balance in Chillingworth. In the meantime, you should realize that Hester is reaching for responsibility, while Chillingworth is trying to evade it. Much of what is said and done in this chapter reflects a very different attitude, on the part of these two characters, toward moral accountability.

Hester now turns to her purpose. She has given Chillingworth a promise of silence that she now regrets. She has left her husband in a position to watch Dimmesdale day and night, to poison the minister's thoughts, to play on his heartstrings. She will retract that promise now.

Chillingworth, at first, denies Hester's accusation. " 'What evil have I done the man?' " Chillingworth asks. Why, no evil at all. In fact, Chillingworth asserts, he has lavished on Dimmesdale medical care fit for a king. It is only thanks to the physician's care that Dimmesdale is still alive.

The argument would be quite convincing, if we didn't know better. But we know, and Hester suspects, that Chillingworth has only been pretending to minister to Dimmesdale's ailments while in reality adding to his distress.

Chillingworth now hurries on to reveal his true intentions, to make explicit the evil within him, and to pass a rather unexpected judgment on himself.

Yes, Dimmesdale has suffered, Chillingworth now

admits. He has suffered hideously, and he has never known why. With monkish superstition, he has imagined himself visited by a fiend.

> "Yea, indeed!—he did not err!—there was a fiend at his elbow! A mortal man, with once a human heart, has become a fiend for his especial torment!"

Well, Chillingworth has said it himself, though we may wonder if fiends are inclined to label themselves for our convenience. He stops in horror at his own words. But the horror leads him not to a reversal of his position but to a recommitment to his ugly methods of revenge.

Contemplating just how far he has fallen from grace, Chillingworth knows there is no turning back. Once he was a decent man, kindly, honest, just. But now he is a hellish creature, given over to another's torment. Like Macbeth, Chillingworth has waded in evil so far that he can't imagine returning to shore. Hester pleads for pardon, but her words are thrown back by the winds. Chillingworth is too far out to sea to hear.

Overwhelmed by a sense of futility, Hester gives way to despair. She will not stoop to plead with such a creature as Chillingworth, even for Dimmesdale's life. She will do as she must. She will go to the minister and reveal her husband's secret, though all the while she will expect the worst. " 'Do with him as thou wilt! There is no good for him,—no good for me,—no good for thee! . . . There is no path to guide us out of this dismal maze!' "

NOTE: Hester's cry of despair is worth stopping for, since it is one of three significant quotes that occur in the short space of a single chapter. All these quotes sound like term paper topics; quick, easy summaries of the meaning of *The Scarlet Letter*.

It is important to remember, under this barrage of aphorisms, that we are reading dramatic dialogue. Hester and Chillingworth are both speaking out of full hearts and under the pressure of the moment.

Chillingworth's eyes light up at the sheer magnificence of Hester's despair. He feels a thrill of admiration for her capacity to look truth so cooly in the face. What a woman, he thinks to himself. And he says (it is the second of those significant quotes), " 'I pity thee, for the good that has been wasted in thy nature.' '

Once again, Chillingworth seems to hit the nail on the head. His words echo within us. They express our fear that Hester has, indeed, lived for nothing—for a few weeks of love, perhaps, and then for the long years of emptiness.

Is Hester a waste? Some readers say yes, appalled at the lonely life which seems so contrary to her passionate nature. Others say no, impressed by the spiritual growth which gives meaning to her existence. You will have to draw your own conclusions, remembering that it is Chillingworth, no trustworthy critic, who has called Hester a waste in the first place.

Chillingworth closes the chapter with a moral shrug of the shoulders. He cannot change, he will not pardon. For the desperate straits in which he, Hester, and Dimmesdale now find themselves, there is really no one to blame. It has all been fate, or (here comes that third quote) "dark necessity."

What does Chillingworth mean? He is referring to a dark, fatalistic strain in Puritanism, the idea that we are all damned or saved by God, even before we are born. Since our future is predetermined, Chillingworth is saying, why worry about it? We do what we are destined to do.

Now the Puritans *did* believe in predestination. But they never for a moment argued that we are therefore absolved of the obligation to live the best possible lives. In fact, they insisted on quite the reverse: goodness and morality every waking minute.

Chillingworth is being heretical in his views. But you don't need to be a religious expert to question Chillingworth's opinion. You only need common sense. Chillingworth *wants* to believe that it is impossible for him to pardon. And so, he goes to his religion for a doctrine to confirm his desire.

CHAPTER 15: HESTER AND PEARL

Watching Chillingworth depart, all but scorching the countryside as he goes, Hester makes one of the private judgments that mark her lately as an independent thinker: " 'Be it sin, or no,' . . . 'I hate the man!' "

She wrestles with the thought for a moment, because she knows she has no business hating anyone, especially a man she has wronged. Moreover, she has just described pardon to Chillingworth as a "priceless benefit." She knows she should be searching for that golden vein of forgiveness within herself. But the bitter memories that come flooding in are too strong for Christian doctrine.

Hester recalls with something close to horror the early days of her marriage, when she and Chillingworth would sit by the fire, exchanging smiles that represented lukewarm affection, perhaps, but surely not love.

She believes it her own worst sin that she consented to a marriage of contentment—or worse, convenience. And she judges it Chillingworth's foulest crime that he cheated her, when she was too young to know better, into thinking herself happy at his side.

As you read this description of Hester's thoughts, you may feel that, at long last, she has come into her own. She has ceased to struggle with imposed morality (hate may be sin, but she doesn't care). And she is finally confronting the truth of her own emotions. The Puritans may have condemned her for adultery, but her real sin (as she now believes) lay in being false to herself.

On the other hand, you may feel that the force of Hester's emotion has thrown her off balance. After all, she has just turned all her previously held moral convictions upside down. In only the last chapter, Hester accepted responsibility for Chillingworth's deterioration. Now she is blaming him for her own mistakes. " 'He betrayed me!' " she says to herself. " 'He has done me worse wrong than I did him!' "

What has caused Hester to swing in this wide circle? Perhaps we should see in her sudden fierce condemnation of Chillingworth no moral conclusion at all, but the passionate reaction of a woman who has suddenly realized she is still in love with another man.

Whatever you decide about Hester's state of mind—whether you think she is being true to herself or false to something better—you should realize that the very next thing she does is to lie. And lie to her daughter, whom she loves, on a subject of great importance.

Pearl has, as usual, been thinking about the scarlet letter and incorporating it in her games. But this time, there is a special earnestness in her manner that makes Hester wonder whether Pearl has reached the age to be trusted with some of the truth. Holding her mother's hand and looking with unusual thoughtfulness into her mother's eyes, Pearl asks the two questions that have troubled her all her life: What does the scarlet letter mean? And why does the minister keep his hand over his heart?

Hester hesitates, tempted to tell her daughter something of the story of her sin. But at the last moment, she backs down. She gives the child a shamefully false and silly answer. Hester tells Pearl she wears the scarlet letter for decoration, for the "sake of its golden thread."

Pearl, of course, knows she has been lied to. The sympathy and earnestness vanish from her face. She becomes a total nuisance on the subject of the letter, never letting the matter drop.

Pearl repeats her questions day and night until Hester is driven half-mad. Plagued by these constant reminders of her cowardice she threatens to lock the child in a closet.

Hester's unaccustomed harshness suggests she regrets the lost opportunity. The moment of trust and closeness may not come again.

NOTE: Pearl's questions about the scarlet letter, though always on the tip of her tongue, are inspired in this chapter by a green letter *A* that she makes from seaweed found on the beach.

On this occasion Pearl seems to show a child's ignorance, rather than an imp's supernatural intelligence, on the subject of the letter. As Hester points out, the green *A* on Pearl's chest is essentially meaningless. It suggests freshness and innocence, rather than anything smacking of evil or experience.

CHAPTER 16: A FOREST WALK

Having failed to move Chillingworth from his purpose of revenge, Hester decides to seek out Dimmesdale and reveal to the minister himself the true character of the physician.

She has learned that Dimmesdale has gone to visit the Apostle Eliot, a missionary among the Indians. She decides to meet the minister in the forest on his homeward journey.

The forest is a very different sort of setting from any we have been reading about. We are far away from the market-place, the safe heart of the settlement. We are deep in the primeval woods where the only sign of humanity is a narrow footpath, hemmed in by the trees.

Perhaps we can view "A Forest Walk" as a stage director's efforts to create a set and arrange the lighting for the crisis of his play. The forest will shortly be the setting for a love scene, a setting as wild and as fundamental as the passion that seeks its shelter.

The forest, we should note, shows different faces to different people. To Hester, the woods are dark and somber, but she welcomes the darkness as an assurance of privacy. She has come here to meet Arthur Dimmesdale far away from prying eyes.

To Pearl, the forest is a friendly place. The brook babbles to her like a playmate. The sun caresses her, finding in her brightness and gaiety a spirit that matches its own.

NOTE: The fickle rays of sunshine follow Pearl, but flee from Hester because of the scarlet letter. The letter shows that Hester carries into nature a burden of guilt imposed by civilization. Society's token is not recognized in the woods. In the great realm of nature, it is the insignia of a foreign power.

To the Puritans, as Pearl reminds us, the forest has a darker significance. Here witches dance among the trees, and the devil walks abroad to claim souls for his own.

Pearl is, of course, repeating an old wives' tale, a story she has heard from a withered crone, huddled in the chimney corner for warmth on a cold spring night. But is the story just an old wives' tale? Or does it hold a kernel of truth?

The forest, we must remember, is free. Nobody watches in the woods to report misbehavior to the magistrates. Here people do as they like. And what they like is breaking rules.

To independent spirits like Hester Prynne's, the wilderness sings a siren's song: "Throw off the shackles of law and religion. What good have they done you anyway? Look at you, a young and vibrant woman, grown old before your time. And no wonder, hemmed in, as you are, on every side by prohibitions. Why, you can hardly walk without tripping over one commandment or another. Come to me, and be masterless."

Hester will soon respond to that wild note of the forest. But she gives no sign of hearing it yet.

In the meantime, we discover, Pearl has heard more than a general tale of devils and witches from that old crone in the chimney corner. She has heard a very specific reference in the story to her mother. Is it true, Pearl asks, that the scarlet letter is the Black Man's mark? And does it glow red at night when Hester meets him in the forest?

Hester responds to Pearl's question with one of her own: Has Pearl ever awakened at night and found her mother gone from the cottage?

It is possible that Hester is being evasive, answering one question with another. But more likely, she is claiming simple justice from her daughter. We remember that Hester has, in fact, been invited to the forest by Mistress Hibbins. And she declined the invitation, choosing instead to stay at home with Pearl.

In any case, Pearl will not be put off; she repeats her questions. And this time, Hester does not lie to her daughter. She answers with something at least like the truth. " 'Once in my life I met the Black Man! . . . The scarlet letter is his mark!' "

Does Hester believe what she is saying? Or is she only agreeing to this version of her story because it is an explanation that Pearl can understand? Hester will have a different tale to tell in the next chapter, one we will have to measure against this.

CHAPTER 17: THE PASTOR AND HIS PARISHIONER

After carefully setting the scene in "A Forest Walk," Hawthorne brings us to the long-awaited meeting of Hester Prynne and Arthur Dimmesdale. It is a reunion that will span the next three chapters and provide the most dramatic and heart-rending moments of the novel.

Seven years have passed since the lovers have met in private, years that have taken a frightful toll on the minister, even as they have strengthened and disciplined Hester.

Not surprisingly, the two find a kind of unreality in the moment. They see each other through a mist that only clears with the chill touch of Dimmesdale's hand on Hester's.

Hawthorne tells us that it took a lot of small talk—remarks about the weather and so on—before Hester and Dimmesdale could open up to each other. But small talk is not what we hear. Only questions and answers of stunning simplicity: " 'Art thou in life?' " " 'Hast thou found peace?' "

Perhaps we can learn something about the characters' state of mind by looking at those questions, one at a time.

" 'Art thou in life?' " " 'And thou, Arthur Dimmesdale, dost thou yet live?' " Hester may mean something rather different by this first question than Dimmesdale does. The minister has been far too wrapped up in himself to keep tabs on Hester. He has seen her only once in recent years, the night of his vigil on the scaffold, when she appeared like an image summoned by this thought. He really does not know whether she is still alive.

Hester, on the other hand, has had good reason to be anxious about the minister's health. She has just seen him collapsed upon a bed of forest leaves. Her question really means, does Dimmesdale still have the strength to live.

" 'Hast thou found peace?' " Hester believes this second question deserves only a dreary smile and a passing nod to the scarlet letter—that emblem of torture—on her breast. But Dimmesdale seizes the occasion to relieve himself, at some length and to the only possible listener, of the agony that has been eating away at his heart.

He is weary unto death of his false position, he tells Hester. He is doubtful of the efficacy of his work and bitter in his soul at the contrast between what he is and what he seems. " 'Of penance, I have had enough! Of penitence, there has been none!' " he says, rather neatly expressing the difference between the futile acts of contrition he has taken up and the real change of heart he has never yet experienced. (Dimmesdale is an orator with a gift for the nicely turned phrase.)

Dimmesdale then gives Hester the opening she is looking for. If only he had a friend—or even an enemy—who recognized him for what he was, the worst of sinners. To see himself truthfully reflected in just one pair of eyes a day might save him.

Hester has come to the forest expressly to tell Dimmesdale that he has such an enemy. She speaks her piece now, though with great trepidation. She believes that her deception of the minister has been a dire wrong. As she confesses it, she throws herself, in an unusually demonstrative gesture, at Dimmesdale's feet.

Dimmesdale does not come off well in the next few moments. He turns to Hester in anger, accusing her of nothing short of betrayal. The raging minister tells Hester she has left him indecently exposed to his enemy. Thanks to her, his suffering has been witnessed by the very eye that would gloat over it.

Dimmesdale might have remembered that Hester has had her own trials to bear, trials in which *he* offered *her* no aid.

But Dimmesdale's fit of anger passes, leaving him quieter than before. He is now willing to make a kinder judgment on both Hester and himself. " 'We are not, Hester, the worst sinners in the world. There is one worse than even the polluted priest! That old man's revenge has been blacker than my sin. He has violated, in cold blood, the sanctity of a human heart.' "

It is characteristic of Dimmesdale that, smack in the middle of a love scene, he can make us stop and think. In his priestly way, he has just made a comparative moral judgment, one to be weighed and measured. Dimmesdale is saying that Chillingworth is guilty of a premeditated crime. The old man has turned the cold light of his intellect on human suffering and, what's more, has sought to increase it. Dimmesdale's sin, on the contrary, is the result of runaway passion. Once desire overcame his scruples as a clergyman. And since then, cowardice has taken over.

For once, guided by Hester and not by Chillingworth, Dimmesdale can see the human element in his situation. He can offer himself a small measure of forgiveness.

Hester confirms Dimmesdale's judgment. But, as usual, she pushes the minister further than he is ready to go. " 'What we did . . .' " she reminds him, " 'had a consecration of its own. We felt it so! We said so to each other!' " Dimmesdale, frightened as much by Hester's audacity as by the memory of those heady days, tells her (not for the last time in the novel) to hush.

Hester and Dimmesdale sit quietly for a while, grateful for this brief respite in their troubles. The path lies before them back to the settlement where Hester must take up her burden of shame and Dimmesdale his life of hypocrisy. But not yet. They linger in the gray twilight of the forest, charmed by the novelty of letting go, of laying down the guards they carry before the world.

Dimmesdale is the first to break the spell. He comes back to reality with a start. What, he asks Hester, is he to do about Chillingworth? Now that he knows the physician's true identity, he can no longer live under the same roof with the man. But then, he sees no escape except to crawl under the leaves and die.

The deterioration in Dimmesdale becomes evident now. He is childish in his confusion, too weak to make the most basic decisions about life. He turns to Hester as a small boy might turn to his mother, placing all responsibility in her hands. " 'Be thou strong for me,' " he pleads. " 'Advise me what to do.' "

Hester is appalled by her lover's disintegration, but she accepts the opportunity his weakness provides. Perhaps she feels that if she cannot have a man, she can at least have her way. She starts to exercise what Hawthorne calls "a magnetic power" over Dimmesdale's shattered spirit.

Is Hester manipulating Dimmesdale and taking unfair advantage of his moral collapse? Or is she legitimately seeking to put heart into her lover? It is hard to be sure. Whatever Hester's purpose, she makes one of the most moving and eloquent speeches any woman has ever made to the man she loves.

Don't lie there and talk about dying, Hester tells Dimmesdale. Pick yourself up and go. Go out into the wilderness or over the sea to England, and build yourself a new life. Don't be deceived by this false appearance of doom. See farther, and see with my eyes. You say the forest track leads back to the settlement. Well, so it does. But it goes on from there. Deeper and deeper into the wilderness, until all signs of civilization vanish. There you will be free of Chillingworth and free, too, of the guilt that has been eating away at your heart.

It is a magnificent speech, a clarion call to freedom. And in it, Hester has captured the whole premise of America. The New World meant precisely escape from the past, one's own past included. What Hester holds forth to Dimmesdale is what the frontier offered every man: a shining vision of a new life, waiting somewhere just to the west, where the grass glistens in the morning dew as if in the first sunrise of the world.

Yes, it is a magnificent speech, but one we should read with caution. For Hester's speech raises two questions that are absolutely central to *The Scarlet Letter:* Is escape from the past possible? And even if possible, is escape an ethically acceptable choice?

NOTE: Hester's speech bears a remarkable resemblance to one of Dimmesdale's own sermons. The verbs are overwhelmingly commands. " 'Begin all anew!' . . . 'Preach! Write! Act!' "

The rhetorical devices, too, are those a minister might use to sway a doubtful audience. The questions, for example, seem to have obvious answers, but when properly considered, they yield unexpected and illuminating insights. " 'Whither leads yonder forest-track? Backward to the settlement, thou sayest! Yea; but onward, too! Deeper it goes, and deeper, into the wilderness . . . until, some few miles hence, the yellow leaves will show no vestige of the white man's tread.' "

We remember that the chapter is called "The Pastor and His Parishioner," and we appreciate the irony of the title now. The roles of pastor and parishioner are reversed. Dimmesdale is seeking guidance, and Hester is giving it, with all the skill of a Puritan divine.

To Dimmesdale, Hester's vision of the future seems like a dream. Perhaps he has an inkling of the truth, that the wilderness will hold for him only what he brings to it. And he can bring very little now.

Dimmesdale protests that he is too weak to start a new life. He has moral objections, too. He would feel like a sentry deserting his post.

But his protests are feeble. He is all the while angling for something. Twice he says to Hester that he is unable to consider such a venture *alone*.

Hester is at the starting gate, waiting for him. It is the invitation, even if only half-expressed, that she has been hoping for.

She whispers to her minister, " 'Thou shalt not go alone!' "

CHAPTER 18: A FLOOD OF SUNSHINE

" 'Thou shalt not go alone.' " Hester's words echo in Dimmesdale's mind. His heart leaps with joy, but hypocrite that he is, he is appalled at Hester's boldness in speaking out loud what he himself has barely hinted at.

Nonetheless, Dimmesdale decides to go, a decision over which Hawthorne draws a curtain of silence. Let us peer beneath the curtain for a moment and see if we can figure out what is on Dimmesdale's mind. Then we'll go back and see what Hawthorne actually says.

Dimmesdale, as we know, is in no shape for a calm and rational decision. He is exhausted and emotionally overwrought. He is wide open to the power of suggestion. He will grasp at any solution Hester offers him.

And what does Hester offer him? Something very much like escape from death row. Dimmesdale must feel, at this point, rather like a man who has been imprisoned in a dungeon for years. Suddenly, a guard appears and unbolts the door. The guard says—the words are like music to the prisoner's ears—"It is all a mistake. You are free to go."

Such a prisoner might doubt his senses for a while. But he would not send the guard back to check on his release. He would not ask too many questions either. He would stand on his wobbly legs and go.

In effect, that is what Dimmesdale does. And Hawthorne now has a few things to say. At this point in the chapter, the author breaks into the flow of the narrative to provide a commentary on what has taken place.

The section of commentary begins with the second paragraph ("But Hester Prynne, with a mind of native courage. . . .") and continues for four paragraphs more (through ". . . the clergyman resolved to flee, and not alone"). It is a section that has caused problems to many a reader.

Problem 1: In the middle of a love scene, this section seems dry and analytical. We have just been carried away on the wings of Hester's enthusiasm. And here is Hawthorne, calling us back down to earth. Problem 2: After the warmth and emotive power of the dialogue, the section is preachy and didactic. It is a sermon, if you like, to counter Hester's own.

Hawthorne wants to explain, it seems, that all that wonderful rhetoric of Hester's was really just the talk of a renegade. Society has outlawed Hester Prynne. As a result, she has wandered "without rule or guidance, in a moral wilderness." Hester has been set free as a savage to criticize all that is sacred in religion, all that is venerable in law. We can admire Hester's courage, Hawthorne tells us, for daring to venture into intellectual wastelands like these. But we cannot admire her conclusions. Her conclusions are wrong.

If Hawthorne is critical of Hester, he is much rougher on Dimmesdale. For running away from his responsibilities, the minister has not a shadow of an excuse. Unlike Hester, Dimmesdale has never been left to his own moral devices. The best we can say of him is that—weakened by guilt, confused by remorse—he chooses open flight over a life of sham.

What are we to make of this tidy moral lecture thrust into the middle of the forest scene? Some readers simply dismiss it. Hawthorne, they say, is really on the lovers' side, but he's worried about offending the tender sensibilities of his Victorian readers. So he throws in this little critique of illicit passion just to be on the safe side.

Other readers latch on to this moral lecture as *the* meaning of the forest scene. However attractive Hawthorne finds the romantic option, they say, he knows it is wrong. Look: Hawthorne expresses his opinion clearly—in black and white—just so there won't be any mistake.

Still a third group of readers sense a split in Hawthorne himself. The artist in Hawthorne—the Romantic half, let us say—sympathizes with the lovers and recognizes the claims of emotional intensity. But the moralist in Hawthorne—or the Puritan half—believes that passion justifies nothing and that giving into it is sin.

You will have to decide where you think Hawthorne stands, weighing the drama of the forest scene against the didacticism, the force of the lovers' passion against their perilous moral position. But not just yet, for Hawthorne has returned to his story.

We rejoin the narrative to find Dimmesdale lifted up on a wave of joy. Surely, he feels, such happiness must have a blessing on it. He has flung himself down, "sin-stained" and "sorrow-blackened" on a bed of leaves. Now he has "risen up, all made anew." The minister feels, in the language of fundamentalist sects, born again—but in love, not in Christ.

Dimmesdale uses religious terms to express his sense of exhilaration. Hester, as we might expect, has a different method. She unpins the scarlet letter from her dress and tosses it toward a nearby stream. (The letter, we note for future reference does not quite make the water. It lands on the bank of the stream.) Hester's gesture is a proclamation: The past is dead and the slate is wiped clean. " 'With this symbol, I undo it all,' " she says, " 'and make it as it had never been!' "

NOTE: You will want to compare Hester's words with those she spoke to Reverend Wilson in the market-place in Chapter 3. Then she told the clergyman that the scarlet letter was too deeply branded to be removed. Was she right then? Or is she right now?

Taking off her cap, Hester unlooses her hair. As the dark strands cascade down her back, she becomes a woman again. Her eyes grow radiant. A flush comes to her cheek. The sensuality of the early chapters returns.

The sunlight, which previously shunned Hester, now seeks her out. In her present state, she is at one with nature. The forest glows in the golden light, rejoicing with the lovers, sharing their mood.

We sense that something vitally important has happened in this scene, a possibility barely even hinted at before. Hester and Dimmesdale have come to life again. The minister, half-dead when he first lay down in the forest, is buoyed up, hopeful, energetic. The woman of marble that was Hester Prynne only a few pages ago is now all tenderness and fire.

We are, of course, swept away. As the saying goes, everybody loves a lover. And who could resist such lovers as these, lit up like Christmas trees after years of darkness?

And yet, we may suspect it is all too easy. As Dimmesdale himself wonders, if the high road to freedom has always been open, why have they not taken it before? There is a hitch in this beautiful scheme of theirs. The hitch is Pearl.

CHAPTER 19: THE CHILD AT THE BROOK-SIDE

Hester turns to Dimmesdale, saying it is high time he knew his daughter. Pearl has wandered off in the woods somewhere. She is busy picking flowers and playing with small animals: squirrels, partridges, and the like.

Dimmesdale, we notice, is hardly the proud father that Hester might have hoped. Selfish as always, he worries that people may have noticed the striking resemblance between Pearl and himself. Hester, who knows how to handle her nervous lover, soothingly reminds him that, in a little while, he need not be afraid to be recognized as Pearl's father.

The minister, however, is still jumpy. Children are not at ease with him, he says. They never volunteer to kiss him or climb on his knee. (And we can see why. He is just the kind of man to complain about noise when he is trying to study, or a spot on his shirt left by a child's sticky hands. Men like Dimmesdale are not born for fatherhood.)

In the meantime, Pearl has come back.

As the child approaches, Hester and Dimmesdale are struck by her wild beauty. Decked out with flowers, Pearl resembles a native spirit of the forest.

When Pearl stops by the bank of the stream, she is reflected in a pool of water, so that there are two Pearls, both shimmering in the gloom. The double image has a kind of unreality. And Hester is seized by the fancy that Pearl has wandered off into another world, on the far side of the brook, where she will be forever cut off from her mother.

Hester's idea proves to be no fancy at all but nothing short of the truth. Pearl stubbornly refuses to obey her mother's command to jump across the stream and make friends with the minister.

Instead, the child points an accusing finger at the vacant spot on Hester's dress. She frowns, she stamps her foot. And when Hester begins to scold, Pearl throws herself into wild contortions and utters piercing shrieks that echo through the forest.

It is all too much for Dimmesdale's nerves. He begs Hester to do something—anything—fast. Hester has no choice but to pacify Pearl. She knows what the child misses, and she wades into the stream to retrieve the scarlet letter.

What is happening in this scene? On a narrative level, Pearl is behaving like the petted and spoiled child she is. She is furious to find herself faced with a rival claimant to her mother's affections. She understands that the change in Hester's appearance signals a new state of affairs—one she heartily dislikes. She registers her disapproval by means of a temper tantrum.

On a symbolic level, Pearl is acting out the role of a fierce little nemesis. Her pointing finger is the accusing finger of fate. Pearl's mission in life has always been to remind Hester of the consequences of sin. She will not let her mother escape those consequences now.

Pearl's silent message, as she stands there on the far side of the stream, is that there is no return from experience to innocence. She will not recognize her mother until the scarlet letter is once more in place and Hester's luxuriant hair, that radiant sign of young womanhood, is once more imprisoned beneath the restraining cap.

Do you find something cruel in Pearl, something merciless in her insistence that Hester forego her newfound youth and sensuality? Perhaps Hawthorne does, too. But the cruelty lies not so much in the child as in the situation. Hawthorne believes that there is something final and irrevocable about sin. But he does not necessarily love the Providence that has decreed it so.

Pearl is now willing to greet her mother, but she will have nothing to do with the minister. When Dimmesdale plants a nervous kiss on her forehead, she runs back to the stream to wash it off.

Hester and Dimmesdale draw aside to discuss their plans for the future. But we know now, for we have just been warned: this is a marriage that will never come off.

CHAPTER 20: THE MINISTER IN A MAZE

Dimmesdale returns home from the forest to the settlement. As we watch him go, we are struck by the change in the man. The minister who went to the woods was weak to the point of death. The minister who returns is nothing short of frenzied. In fact, he seems a little mad.

Dimmesdale's journey home is a progress fraught with peril, for at every step, he is tempted to do some outrageous thing or other: preach heresy to his deacon, corrupt an innocent girl, teach dirty words to children, exchange lusty oaths with a sailor.

The minister is terrified and amazed at himself. What, he wonders, has happened to him?

What, indeed?

You may take a modern, psychological view of Dimmesdale's case. You may decide he's simply been living too long under a rigid form of self-restraint. Seeing Hester was like lifting the lid off a boiling pot. It isn't surprising that the man is letting off steam. If you take this view, you will probably be somewhat indulgent toward Dimmesdale. After all, some of the actions he envisions are really only schoolboy pranks.

On the other hand, you may see Dimmesdale's crisis in religious or moral terms. If so, you will probably accept Hawthorne's statement of the case. Dimmesdale, having chosen what he knew to be sin, is becoming every minute more of a sinner. The minister is on a roller coaster ride in hell. Having once mounted the infernal machine, he careens onward, powerless to get off.

This latter interpretation receives some support from Dimmesdale's encounter with Mistress Hibbins. Devil's familiar that Hibbins is, she now recognizes in Dimmesdale a kindred spirit. A little bird has told her, apparently, that the minister has signed his name in the Black Man's ironbound book.

Now, we have learned to trust Mistress Hibbins' opinion. Long ago, in front of the Governor's mansion, she spotted in Hester a likely candidate for the wild forest dance. And sure enough once Hester got to the forest, her demure appearance vanished. Her hair tumbled down and a wild light shone in her eyes.

Yet, Mistress Hibbins' "hail-fellow-well-met" greeting to the minister raises a question. Are we really supposed to see the forest meeting of the lovers as some sort of infernal pact with Hester in the role of evil temptress? If we balk at this construction of events, it is only the beginning of our troubles. We come smack up against another dilemma in the minister's newfound strength.

If Dimmesdale has indeed sold his soul to the devil, he has come out ahead in the bargain. When he was "good," he was weak and lethargic; good, perhaps, but certainly good for nothing. Now that he is "bad," he is energetic, ready for action, capable of doing something, if only of raising hell.

In Dimmesdale's behavior, Hawthorne has sensed a truth that has (for him) chilling implications. The minister's energy sources are closely linked to his sensuality. When the sap rises in the man, he is raring to go. But passion, Hawthorne has said (see "The Pastor and His Parishioner"), is the part of Dimmesdale the devil claimed. Only the higher, purer qualities are directed toward God.

Is the choice, then, between a virtuous torpor and an active, creative evil? For Dimmesdale? For all of us? If so, it is the devil's own choice.

Hawthorne now brings Dimmesdale home where he does two interesting things. First, he lies like a trooper to Chillingworth, concealing (if has any hopes of concealing) the knowledge of Chillingworth's true position that Dimmesdale has gained from Hester Prynne. Here is a change from Dimmesdale's old simplicity, the sign of the serpent upon him, indeed.

But the minister does something else, something that points in a different direction. He begins anew that piece of work which is so important to him, the Election Sermon. He channels, almost by accident, the dubious energy sparked by the forest meeting into his true calling, the saving of souls. He works like a man inspired (or a man possessed) until the next morning, when the sermon lies finished before him on the study floor.

CHAPTER 21: THE NEW ENGLAND HOLIDAY

In this chapter, Hawthorne shows us a lighter side of Puritanism. We have come to think of these first colonists as unreservedly gloomy. Here we find them in a brighter, gayer mood.

We come upon the colonists in a highly unusual act: celebrating. To mark the election of new magistrates, the colony has set aside its work. The citizens of Boston have gathered in the market-place to make merry as best they can. There is a parade planned, with music, and wrestling matches, too.

Hester and Pearl are part of the celebration. Though Hester stands on the sidelines, wearing her usual austere dress and her usual stony expression, the note of celebration echoes in her heart. Beneath her poker face, Hester is exultant. She has come to the market-place, she imagines, wearing the scarlet letter for the last time. She silently invites the crowd of spectators to look their last on her badge of shame. In a little while, the letter will lie at the bottom of the sea. And Boston won't have Hester Prynne to kick around any more.

Hester has made plans to leave the colony that very day. She has booked passage for Dimmesdale, Pearl, and herself on a ship, now berthed in the harbor, that is due to sail for England with the evening tide.

Yes, Hester is triumphant, but her triumph is premature. The holiday mood of the market-place is deceptive, so far as she is concerned. As Hester speaks to the shipmaster, she discovers that Chillingworth has booked passage on the same boat. The leech will stick to his patient all the way to England. There will be no shaking him off.

Hester is shaken by the shipmaster's news. As she digests this unwelcome piece of information, she catches sight of Chillingworth on the other side of the square. He is watching her across the mass of gaily chattering people. On his face, he wears the implacable smile of fate.

CHAPTER 22: THE PROCESSION

We are still in the market-place. There is a lot going on to catch our eye.

We see the magistrates on parade: firm, stalwart men who in times of peril have stood up to protect the colony like rocks against the tide.

We see Pearl in her bright red dress, flitting among the spectators like a great wild bird. She is wilder in her nature, we are reminded, than the pirates and the Indians whom she runs to inspect with her childish curiosity.

But our attention is really fixed on Hester—or rather on Hester watching Dimmesdale as he passes by in the procession. This is not the man she left in the woods. His step is firm and energetic now. And he is as indifferent to her presence as if he were a million miles away. Not a glance, not a nod of recognition does he give her. And this is on the eve of their planned escape! Hester is crushed and desolate as she watches her lover retreat into that private world of his own, where she cannot follow him.

Dimmesdale's preoccupied air is also noticed by Mistress Hibbins, who corners Hester for an intimate little chat. Now who would believe, the old witch asks, that this saintly minister, who looks as if his head has been buried in his books for months on end, has in fact just returned from an airing in the woods?

How does she know, wonders a startled Hester. It is a question we also ask ourselves. And we're about to get an answer. In a moment, Mistress Hibbins will reveal the source of her privileged information.

When Hester protests that she cannot speak lightly of the pious Mr. Dimmesdale, Mistress Hibbins turns on her indignantly. Come on, Hester, she says, don't lie to me. Do you really think I've been to the forest so many times and can't tell who else has been there, even if no tell-tale twigs or leaves still cling to their hair?

What the old witch is saying is that she needs no black magic to see into the minister's heart. Experience itself is an eye-opener. Mistress Hibbins can read guilty thoughts in other people because she has had them herself, and so she recognizes the symptoms: a certain spring to the walk, perhaps, or a certain gleam in the eye. The forest leaves its mark on everyone, witches and ministers alike.

Mistress Hibbins bursts into shrill laughter and walks away. Hester draws near the meeting house to hear Dimmesdale's Election Sermon. As the place is packed, she stands outside by the scaffold of the pillory, listening to the rise and fall of Dimmesdale's voice.

Does Hester understand Dimmesdale's meaning, even though she cannot hear the words? Most likely, for she is in complete sympathy with her lover. She has not withdrawn from him, as he has from her. And what she hears is " . . . the complaint of a human heart, sorrow-laden, perchance guilty, telling its secret . . . to the great heart of mankind."

CHAPTER 23: THE REVELATION

Dimmesdale's Election Sermon is the triumph of his life. The crowd in the market-place is ecstatic. Never has a preacher been so inspired. The spirit of prophecy has lifted Dimmesdale to new heights from which he foretold a glorious future for the people of New England.

Yet it is a future that their minister will not share. The citizens of Boston sense that Dimmesdale is dying. He has spoken like an angel ascending to heaven, who has shaken his wings and sent down "a shower of golden truths" upon them.

Hawthorne is being ironic, but his irony has a tragic edge. Dimmesdale is no angel, but he is a dying man. He has carefully nurtured his strength to get through the Election Sermon. But now that it is over, he is as limp as a rag doll. He staggers, he totters, but he keeps himself on his feet. Before he dies, he has a job to do.

Dimmesdale approaches the scaffold and calls out to Hester and Pearl to join him. The child flies to his side, for this is the public sign of recognition that she has been waiting for.

Hester moves slowly, unwillingly, forward. She knows what is coming. She is about to lose her lover a second time. And this time, the pain is sharper because it is unexpected. He has come so tantalizingly within reach, and now he is about to vanish—forever.

Chillingworth is equally surprised and appalled by Dimmesdale's obvious intention. He rushes forward to stop the minister from making a public confession. If Hester is losing a lover, he is losing a victim. He cannot play on Dimmesdale's secret guilt once it is no longer secret.

Chillingworth makes a last, frantic appeal to the minister's cowardice (or to his common sense). Dimmesdale's life and honor can still be saved, the physician assures him, if only he will stop now.

Dimmesdale, however, brushes Chillingworth aside. He is no longer listening. He is living on another plane now. He no longer sees a man before him, but only the evil the man represents. " 'Ha, tempter.' " the minister answers, addressing both Chillingworth and the Prince of Darkness he serves, " 'Methinks thou art too late.' "

Dimmesdale stretches forth his hand to Hester to ask for her support. He no longer has the strength to mount the scaffold alone. But now that he has brought himself to the brink of confession, he hesitates. " 'Is this not better . . . than what we dreamed of in the forest?' " he asks. It is a real question, not a rhetorical one, for the minister's eyes are filled with anxiety and doubt.

What does Dimmesdale expect Hester to say? If he is waiting for a nod of approval from her, he has the wrong customer. Hester is the last person on earth to say that death is better than life, that sorrow and repentance are better than love and happiness. Much as she loves Dimmesdale, much as she may be tempted to ease his last moments, she cannot bring herself to call his choice anything but selfish. Better? she says.

Yes, it's better, provided we both die and Pearl along with us.

It's all very well for you to confess, Hester is telling Dimmesdale. You won't have to face the consequences. But what about me? What about Pearl? There's no escape for us now. When you are gone, we'll still be left to pay the piper.

Nevertheless, she gives Dimmesdale her arm. The minister, supported by Hester and Pearl, climbs to the wooden platform where he confesses his sin to the people of Boston. It is a dramatic speech with an unforgettable ending. As the minister concludes, he tears away the cloth that covers his chest and reveals to the crowd the mark, shaped like a letter *A*, which has eaten into his flesh.

The market-place is in tumult. But on the scaffold, Dimmesdale is calm. He turns to Pearl to ask for the kiss she refused him in the forest. The child complies. As she leans her face toward her father's, a great change comes over her. She is truly touched for the first time in her young life. The wicked imp vanishes, replaced by a little girl with a heart.

Hester, having lost the lifetime she planned with Dimmesdale, now bargains for second best. Will they at least share eternity together? she asks her lover urgently. Dimmesdale is once again frightened by Hester's audacity. Hush, he tells her (for the second time in three days). Remember we have sinned. God is merciful, but perhaps not that merciful. Better not to look ahead. Better not to ask too much.

Dimmesdale sacrifices many things—love, life, honor—to make his peace with God. Does he find the peace he is looking for? We read his last words, and we wonder. " 'The law was broke!—the sin here so awfully revealed!—let these alone be in thy thoughts! I fear! I fear!' " The minister makes a statement of faith. He leaves his fate to God. But he turns to heaven at the end darkly, doubtfully.

CONCLUSION

Are conclusions supposed to wrap things up? This one surely doesn't. In fact, it raises more questions than it answers. Perhaps that is the only fit ending for a novel that has never invited us to be complacent.

Let's see what happens to the central characters after Dimmesdale's confession and his death. In the first place, there is some disagreement about the meaning of Dimmesdale's last actions. Some observers of the scaffold scene deny the minister's guilt. They say there was no mark on his chest and that he died in Hester's arms to show that we are all sinners alike. Hawthorne, thank God, doesn't support that view. If he seriously asked us to consider it, we wouldn't know what to think.

Chillingworth dies, too. Well, that is no surprise. He has built his life around Dimmesdale's, trained all his energies on tormenting the minister, and now he has nothing left. So Chillingworth shrivels up and blows away with the wind.

In his will, however, Chillingworth names Pearl as his heir. Pearl! The daughter of Hester Prynne and Arthur Dimmesdale! Now, that is a stunner. Why would Chillingworth want to do a favor for Pearl? Is this a gesture of apology to Dimmesdale, made by the torturer to his victim from the grave? Is it a statement of faith in Hester, a declaration that any daughter of hers must do well, if properly launched in life? Is it an ironic joke, a legacy Chillingworth knows will keep him in Hester's mind forever as an unsolved mystery?

We will never know. But Chillingworth's bequest makes us take another long, hard look at a character we thought we had all sewn up.

Pearl, floated by wealth, sails to Europe where she marries well. She is one of the first American heiresses to trade money for a title. In later centuries, especially Hawthorne's own, it became common practice for the daughters of American millionaires to save the noble houses of Europe with hefty infusions of dollars. We can imagine how this girl, who never minded her manners even in Boston, fared in the far more formal European courts.

Having seen Pearl nicely settled, Hester returns to New England where she resumes the scarlet letter. Now, we can easily understand why Hester leaves a beloved daughter abroad and comes home. Boston is the place where her life has been the fullest—where she has loved Dimmesdale, lost him, and buried him.

But why, once rid of the scarlet letter, does she take up the hated token and wear it again, when nobody tells her to? (Interesting that she never pitched it into the sea, as she promised to.) Does Hester wear the letter now in acceptance of self-restraint, in a long-delayed affirmation of society's sentence upon her?

Maybe. Maybe not.

We have seen Hester once before in the novel clutch the scarlet letter to herself with a fierce mixture of despair and pride. (Way back in the market-place, she told the magistrates that they would never take the letter from her.) Hester's gesture is quieter now, but its meaning may be much the same. The scarlet letter is the symbol of Hester's difference from all the people around her. It is a sign not only of sin but of freedom. The letter marks Hester as one of life's wounded, but it also says, to those who have eyes to see, that here is someone who has dared to live passionately, beyond the limits of society's sad little rules.

When Hester dies, she is buried beside Dimmesdale, under a tombstone that serves for both graves. On the tombstone, the letter *A* is engraved like a heraldic device. So much life and suffering have gone into the symbol that the sign of adultery has become a sign of nobility. Hester has earned her coat of arms.

A STEP BEYOND

Tests and Answers

TESTS

Test 1

1. Hester's crime of adultery _____
   A. was greeted with mixed reactions in King's Chapel
   B. made her liable to capital punishment
   C. made her infamous throughout the thirteen colonies

2. Hester and Dimmesdale disagreed on the _____
   A. morality of elopement
   B. power of prayer
   C. possibility of redemption

3. Hester believed that humans have a "right to happiness" and that _____
   A. her love for Dimmesdale was sacred
   B. her child was her salvation
   C. she owed nothing to contemporary morality

4. Chillingworth was willing to violate human and spiritual realities _____
   A. because of his warped interpretation of religion
   B. in pursuit of his egotistical vengeance
   C. because the law and the church had failed him

5. In branding Hester with the scarlet letter, the   _____
   community was
   A. affirming its own self-righteousness
   B. doling out well-reasoned justice
   C. inviting holy retribution

6. Hawthorne adds to the fascination of the   _____
   scarlet letter by telling of
   I. an *A* in the sky
   II. historical sinners who wore similar marks
   of shame
   III. the different ways in which it affected
   people
   A. I and II
   B. I and III
   C. II and III

7. In "The Custom House" introduction,   _____
   Hawthorne
   I. provides authenticity for the scarlet letter
   story
   II. tells us of his New England roots
   III. discusses Puritan frailties
   A. I and II only
   B. II and III only
   C. I, II, and III

8. Good and evil do battle for Dimmesdale's soul   _____
   in the forms of
   A. Pearl and Mistress Hibbins
   B. Hester and Chillingworth
   C. Governor Bellingham and John Wilson

9. A theme (or themes) of the novel is (are)   _____
   I. sin cannot be hidden from God
   II. sinners should fear God's justice
   III. there is nothing more reprehensible than
   adultery

A. I and II only

B. II and III only

C. I, II, and III

10. Hawthorne is helped in the telling of his tale _____
by the

A. public's interest in marital infidelity

B. harshness of the Puritan ethic

C. eloquence of his major characters

11. Describe the forest and the market-place and explain their significance as settings.

12. It has been said that Hawthorne is interested in sin not as a theological subject, but as a psychological force in the lives of the early New England colonists. Describe the psychological effects of sin on one of the major characters in *The Scarlet Letter*.

Test 2

1. Roger Chillingworth's sin was in _____

A. inciting the hatred of the colony toward poor Dimmesdale

B. refusing to stand up for the woman he loved

C. his decision to play God

2. The older Hester Prynne so impressed her _____
neighbors that they were willing to say her scarlet letter stood for

A. Atonement

B. Able

C. Angelic

3. An ironic touch in the novel is seen in _____

A. Hester's ascent and Chillingworth's descent

    B. the colonists' acceptance of Puritan morality

    C. the colonists' cruelty toward little Pearl

4. According to Hawthorne, Hester's exemplary _____ behavior in later life proceeded from

    A. the cumulative effect of her punishment

    B. her desire to emulate Dimmesdale's sacrifice

    C. God's grace in her heart

5. Chillingworth dies, _____

    A. with the knowledge that the sinners would be punished in the next world

    B. having been cheated of his vengeance

    C. after a reluctant apology to the man he had tormented

6. Hawthorne belonged to the Calvinists, who _____ believed that

    A. sinners do not deserve redemption

    B. redemption followed forgiveness

    C. eternal damnation was reserved for atheists

7. Hester's tomb was graced with _____

    A. a scarlet letter

    B. words from a Biblical psalm

    C. the phrase "Rest, rest, perturbed spirit"

8. Chillingworth's goal was to _____

    I. disorganize and corrupt Dimmesdale's spiritual being

    II. ensure Dimmesdale's damnation

    III. keep Dimmesdale from procuring grace through repentance

    A. I and III only

    B. II and III only

    C. I, II, and III

9. The Reverend Dimmesdale's physical _____
problems were
   A. related to his moral crookedness
   B. directly attributable to Chillingworth's
      cruelty
   C. magnified in his own mind

10. Dimmesdale's decision to ascend the scaffold _____
was
    A. decried by old Chillingworth
    B. welcomed by Governor Bellingham
    C. "Heaven's own method of retribution"

11. Analyze the character of Arthur Dimmesdale. Support
your conclusions with evidence from at least three different chapters.

12. Discuss Hawthorne's use of the scarlet letter as an open,
ambiguous symbol.

ANSWERS

Test 1
1. B	2. A	3. A	4. B	5. A	6. B
7. C	8. A	9. A	10. B		

11. The market-place, with its penitential platform, lies at
the heart of society. Here the Puritans demand conformity of Hester Prynne. Here Dimmesdale comes to confirm his acceptance of society's moral vision. In the forest, which lies beyond society's reach, freedom seems
possible. Here nature takes over, and passion is given
full sway.

   The Puritans distrusted the forest. They knew that
evil could flourish there, unchecked by law or religion.
Hawthorne retains that distrust. In *The Scarlet Letter*, the
forest is still the devil's home. (See the discussion of
setting and "A Forest Walk.")

12. You may choose Hester, Dimmesdale, or Chillingworth. Decide how sin changes your character, affects
his or her thoughts, feelings, perceptions.

You will also want to decide whether sin is a positive
or a negative force in your character's life. About Chillingworth, there is little question. About Hester and
Dimmesdale, there is a good deal. If sin isolates Hester,
it also makes her strong. If sin turns Dimmesdale into a
hypocrite, it also gives him the necessary human touch.
(See the discussions of individual characters and,
depending on the character you write about, "Hester at
Her Needle," "Another View of Hester," "Hester and
the Physician," "The Leech," "The Leech and His
Patient," "The Interior of a Heart," "The Minister in a
Maze.")

Here is a sample answer:

Sin is a double-edged sword in the life of Hester
Prynne. The effects of sin on her character are powerful
and formative, but they are also ambivalent.

The first and most obvious effect of sin on Hester is to
isolate her from the community. From the very beginning of the novel, Hester stands alone. On the scaffold
of the pillory—with the scarlet letter on her dress—
Hester is marked as someone apart from the menacing
crowd that represents the society she has outraged by
her crime.

How does Hester feel, labeled as an adulteress, condemned by the angry spectators in the market-place? A
blush of shame on her cheek combines with a flashing
look of defiance. Hester's ambivalent reaction to her
sin, and to society's appraisal of that sin, continues
throughout the book, with defiance growing under the
cloak of shame and repentance.

After the scaffold scene, Hester assumes compliance
with the rigid Puritan code. She looks and acts like
someone trying to atone for her fault. She takes up acts

of charity to the poor and patiently bears their insults. Over the years, she becomes a Sister of Mercy, giving generously of herself to the sick, the dying, the troubled.

But Hester's seeming admission of her sin, and her gestures of penitence, are if not hypocritical at least superficial. She has never "bought" society's assessment of her love as a vile crime. She has said and believed that what she did had a consecration of its own. That never-quite-suppressed belief combines with society's high-handed insults to turn Hester into a rebel.

There is an old proverb that says it is better to be hanged for stealing a sheep than a lamb. That proverb can tell us a lot about Hester. Condemned as a sinner, never permitted to atone for her sin by society, Hester becomes an outlaw in earnest.

Though she continues to sit in her cottage quietly sewing, though she walks the streets of Boston with a patient, down-cast expression on her face, Hester thinks thoughts that are like a dagger pointed at society's heart.

Hester rejects a social code, a religious creed, that permits the cruelty she has endured. She creates a whole rationale—a party platform—for what the Puritans call deadly sin. By the time she meets Dimmesdale in the forest, she is strong enough to turn common morality on its head. She nearly succeeds in convincing the minister that flight from duty, and commitment to a life-long adulterous union, are goods to be reached after and fought for.

Sin, as some critics have pointed out, turns Hester into a beautiful but terrible and polluted goddess, at least while she is young. Do age and Dimmesdale's death change her? Maybe. Maybe not.

Hester's return to Boston in later years and her

resumption of the scarlet letter may be signs of her final acquiescence to society's verdict. Perhaps she is giving repentance one last try. Or perhaps she is wearing the letter in age, as she did in youth, with pride in her difference from other people. Hester's message at the end may be "I am a sinner," a statement made at last with conviction. Or it may be, what it always was, "I am passionate and free."

Test 2

1. C   **2.** B   **3.** A   **4.** C   **5.** B   **6.** A
7. A   **8.** C   **9.** A   **10.** A

11. There are a number of ways to approach a topic like this. You can talk about Dimmesdale as a hypocrite who suffers from hidden sin or as a scholar-recluse who falls out of his ivory tower. You can ask yourself whether Dimmesdale is a better or a worse person than Hester Prynne. Or you can begin by examining the relationship between Dimmesdale and Chillingworth. Whichever way you decide to tackle Dimmesdale, you should look at his speech to Hester in the market-place, his quarrel with Chillingworth in Chapter 11, his moral collapse in the forest, and his confession at the end. (See the discussion of Dimmesdale under *Characters*, and also "The Recognition," "The Leech and His Patient," "The Interior of a Heart," "A Flood of Sunshine," "The Minister in a Maze," and "The Revelation."

12. You will want to trace the shifting meanings of the scarlet letter from its first appearance on Hester's dress to its final aspect on her tombstone. You should ask yourself some questions about the letter, such as: Why is it embroidered with golden thread? Why is it so fascinating to Pearl? Why does Hester try to throw it away in the woods? And why can't she get rid of it? How do different characters in the novel perceive the letter? How do their perceptions change over the years? Think about those questions, and then take a look at the section on *Symbolism*.

Term Paper Ideas

1. Who is the main character in *The Scarlet Letter*, Hester Prynne or Arthur Dimmesdale? Explain.

2. Contrast Dimmesdale and Chillingworth as scholars and men of intellect.

3. Compare Hester and Mistress Hibbins as women on the fringes of society.

4. Hester Prynne: The best or worst citizen of Boston 1642–1649.

5. Roger Chillingworth: Man? Fiend? Or both?

6. Governor Bellingham: A typical Puritan?

7. Discuss the double life of any leading character in the novel.

8. Write an entry in Hester Prynne's diary during any of the years covered by *The Scarlet Letter*.

9. Arthur Dimmesdale: A study in guilt.

10. Chillingworth to Hester: "I pity thee, for the good that has been wasted in thy nature!" Is Hester a waste?

11. Discuss a significant name in *The Scarlet Letter*.

12. Write a legal defense of Roger Chillingworth. Assume Chillingworth does not die but is, instead, called before the court of Massachusetts to answer for his crimes. Make up a legal plea on his behalf.

Further Reading

Titles marked with an asterisk(*) are available in paperback.

CRITICAL WORKS

Feidelson, Charles, Jr. *Symbolism and American Literature.* Chicago: University of Chicago Press, 1953.

Hawthorne, Julian. *Hawthorne and His Circle.* Darby: Folcroft Library Editions, 1903.

Hawthorne, Julian. *Nathaniel Hawthorne and His Wife: A Biography.* Weston, ON: R. West, 1973; first published, 1884.

Hawthorne, ed. A. N. Kaul. (Twentieth Century Views Series). Englewood Cliffs: Prentice-Hall, Inc., 1966.

James, Henry. *Hawthorne.* (English Men of Letters Series). London: Macmillan & Co., Ltd., 1879.

*Lawrence, D. H. *Studies in Classic American Literature.* New York: The Viking Press, 1961; first published 1923.

Levin, Harry. *The Power of Blackness.* New York: Alfred A. Knopf, Inc., 1958.

Lewis, R.W.B. *The American Adam.* Chicago: University of Chicago Press, 1955.

Matthiessen, F. O. *American Renaissance.* New York: Oxford University Press, 1941.

The Scarlet Letter, ed. John C. Gerber. (Twentieth Century Interpretations Series). Englewood Cliffs: Prentice-Hall Inc., 1968.

The Shock of Recognition. "Volume I: The 19th Century," ed. Edmund Wilson. New York: Grosset & Dunlap, 1943.

Stewart, Randall. *Nathaniel Hawthorne: A Biography.* New Haven: Yale University Press, 1948.

Van Doren, Mark. *Hawthorne.* (American Men of Letters Series). Westport: Greenwood Press, 1973; first published 1949.

AUTHOR'S OTHER WORKS

The Blithedale Romance (1852)
The House of the Seven Gables (1851)
The Marble Faun (1860)
Mosses from an Old Manse (1846)
Twice-Told Tales (1837)
Also:
The Portable Hawthorne, ed. Malcolm Cowley. New York:
   Penguin, 1977.

Glossary

Adams, the elder Second President of the United States (1797-1801).

Alcott, Amos Bronson 19th century Transcendentalist philosopher and founder of the vegetarian Utopian community Fruitlands. He was also the father of Louisa May Alcott, author of *Little Women*.

Antinomian A heretic, according to the Puritans; Antinomians believed that God's grace freed men and women from the obligation to follow civil and moral law.

Apple-peru A plant of the nightshade family; in literature, if not in botany, nightshade is always poisonous.

Assabeth A river near Concord.

Bacon, Coke, Noye, and Finch Late 16th-early 17th-century legalists who made major contributions to British common law.

Beadle A minor parish official whose duties included keeping order; here the beadle seems to function as a town-crier.

Bellingham, Governor Governor of Massachusetts on three different occasions during the 1640s, 50s, and 60s. Hawthorne keeps him in office for reasons of economy and simplicity; also, for his sister's sake. One historical source listed Mistress Hibbins, the witch, as Bellingham's sister.

Blackstone, the Reverend Mr. The first settler on the land that later became Boston. He was a church of England man who didn't get along with the Puritans. He sold out and moved away to what is now Rhode Island.

Bradley, Endicott, Dudley All governors or deputy-governors of the young New England colony. Bradley's wife was the Puritan poet, Anne.

Brook Farm   A Utopian experiment that flourished outside of Boston in the 1840s. Hawthorne joined the commune for a year, but left disillusioned. He later made Brook Farm the subject of a novel, *The Blithedale Romance*.

Bunyan's awful doorway   The entrance to hell in Bunyan's *The Pilgrim's Progress*, a popular allegorical work of the late 17th century.

Burdock   A coarse weed with burrs.

Channing, William Ellery   A Unitarian minister and social reformer who was involved in the anti-slavery movement.

Chronicles of England   Holinshed's history of England, written in 1577.

Digby, Sir Kenalm   17th-century chemist and founder of a science circle in Paris.

Election Sermon   A sermon preached after the annual election of magistrates in Boston.

Eliot, the Apostle   A Puritan minister who became a missionary to the Indians.

Emerson, Ralph Waldo   A Transcendentalist philosopher who believed in the virtues of nature and self-reliance. He is an unmentioned presence throughout *The Scarlet Letter*, for it is principally his beliefs that are being tested in the character of Hester Prynne.

First ancestor   William Hathorne, Hawthorne's great-great-great grandfather, who was one of the original founders of Salem. He came to New England with John Winthrop in 1630. (The *w* was added to the name later.)

Geneva cloak   A black cloak worn by members of the Calvinist clergy. Puritanism was an offshoot of Calvinism, which originated in Geneva, Switzerland.

Gossips   Originally friends or close acquaintances, but here perhaps used also in the modern sense of idle chatterers.

Hibbins, Mistress The wife of a wealthy Boston merchant, listed by one historical source known to Hawthorne as the sister of Governor Bellingham. She was hanged as a witch in 1656.

Hutchinson, Ann A religious dissenter who was excommunicated by the Puritans and expelled from Boston in the 1630s.

Irving's Headless Horseman The ghostly figure who frightened the schoolmaster, Ichabod Crane, in Washington Irving's *The Legend of Sleepy Hollow.*

Johnson, Isaac One of Winthrop's original company in 1630. He came to America just a few months before he died. He was the richest man in Boston of his time.

King James Protestant son of Mary, Queen of Scots, who followed Queen Elizabeth on the throne of England. His reign marked the beginning of a creeping decadence in the court that the Puritans heartily disliked.

King's Chapel An 18th-century Boston landmark. Founded in the 1750s, it was the first Episcopal church in America.

Knights Templar Medieval order whose task it was to oversee pilgrims on their way to the holy land.

Lethe The river of forgetfulness in Hades, the Greek underworld.

Longfellow, Henry Wadsworth Popular 19th-century poet and fellow student of Hawthorne at Bowdoin College.

Lord of Misrule Officer of the English court appointed to oversee the Christmas revels. As the name suggests, the revels were an occasion for turning court decorum upside down.

Marry, I trow Truly, I believe.

Miller, General A hero of the War of 1812. When asked if he could take a British battery, the young officer replied, "I'll try, sir."

Nepenthe   A drug thought by the ancient Greeks to cause forgetfulness and loss of pain.

New England Primer   A moralistic little book from which generations of American children learned their ABCs.

Overbury, Sir Thomas   The subject of an infamous 17th-century murder case. He opposed the marriage of Robert Carr to the divorced Frances Howard. He was sent to the Tower of London, where he was poisoned by Lady Howard's agents.

Pequod Wars   A series of raids on the Pequod villages, conducted in 1637 by the Massachusetts settlers, in revenge for the murder of one John Oldham, a member of the colony. Hundreds of Indians were burned alive.

Simples   Medicinal plants.

Sumptuary regulations   Laws of the colony governing expenses, especially for personal luxuries like food and clothing.

Taylor, General   Zachary Taylor was the 12th president of the United States. His election in 1848 cost Hawthorne his job as Surveyor of the Customs.

Thoreau, Henry David   Author of *Walden*. He was a Transcendentalist and a friend of Hawthorne's and other members of the Concord literary circle.

Turner, Ann   A brothel-keeper involved in the murder of Thomas Overbury. She delivered the poison to the Tower of London.

Whig   In Hawthorne's time, the political party opposed to the Democrats.

Wilson, John   A Cambridge scholar who abandoned law in favor of the ministry. He came to America in 1630 and became a teacher at First Church in Boston. Hawthorne presents him as a leader, or senior member, of the Boston clergy.

Winthrop, John Official first Governor of the Massachusetts Bay Colony. He was the acknowledged leader of the
group of Puritans who came to New England in 1630, the
group that included Hawthorne's great-great-great
grandfather.

The Critics

Theme

In *The Scarlet Letter*, passion justifies nothing, while its denial justifies all. The fallen Eden of this world remains fallen; but the sinful priest purges himself by public confession, becomes worthy of his sole remaining way to salvation, death. Even Hester, though sin and suffering have made her an almost magical figure, a polluted but still terrible goddess, must finally accept loneliness and self-restraint instead of the love and freedom she dreamed.

> *Leslie A. Fiedler, "Achievement and Denial"* Twentieth Century Interpretations of The Scarlet Letter, *1968*

> You have your pure-pure young parson Dimmesdale.
> You have your beautiful Puritan Hester at his feet.
> And the first thing she does is to seduce him.
> And the first thing he does is to be seduced.
> And the second thing they do is to hug their sin in secret, and gloat over it, and try to understand.
> Which is the myth of New England.

> *D. H. Lawrence,* Studies in Classic American Literature, *1923*

Puritanism

Hawthorne was morally, in an appreciative degree, a chip off the old block. His forefathers crossed the Atlantic for conscience sake, and it was the idea of the urgent conscience that haunted the imagination of their so-called degenerate successor. The Puritan strain in his blood ran clear—

there are passages in his diaries, kept during his residence in Europe, which might almost have been written by the grimmest of the old Salem worthies.

Henry James, Hawthorne, 1879

Symbolism

"The Custom House" throws light on a theme in *The Scarlet Letter* which is easily overlooked amid the ethical concerns of the book. Every character, in effect, re-enacts "The Custom House" scene in which Hawthorne himself contemplated the letter, so that the entire "romance" becomes a kind of exposition on the nature of symbolic perception. Hawthorne's subject is not only the meaning of adultery but also meaning in general; not only *what* the focal symbol means but also *how* it gains significance.

Charles Feidelson, Jr., Symbolism and American Literature, 1953

Characters

Above all it is Hester Prynne whose passion and beauty dominate every other person, and color each event. Hawthorne has conceived her as he has conceived his scene, in the full strength of his feeling for ancient New England. He is the Homer of that New England, and Hester is its most heroic creature. Tall, with dark and abundant hair and deep black eyes, a rich complexion that makes modern women (says Hawthorne) pale and thin by comparison, and a dignity that throws into low relief the "delicate, evanescent, and indescribable grace" by which gentility in girls has since come to be known, from the very first—and we believe it—she is said to cast a spell over those who behold her.

Mark Van Doren, Hawthorne, 1949